W9-ANH-433

THE LORD OF THE RINGS

The Mythology of Power

✛

TWAYNE'S MASTERWORK STUDIES

Robert Lecker, General Editor

THE LORD OF THE RINGS

The Mythology of Power

✦

Jane Chance

TWAYNE PUBLISHERS ♦ NEW YORK

Maxwell Macmillan Canada ♦ Toronto

Maxwell Macmillan International ♦ New York Oxford Singapore Sydney

Twayne's Masterwork Studies No. 99

Twayne Publishers   Maxwell Macmillan Canada, Inc.
Macmillan Publishing Company   1200 Eglinton Avenue East
866 Third Avenue   Suite 200
New York, New York 10022   Don Mills, Ontario M3C 3N1

Macmillan Publishing Company is a part of the Maxwell Communication
Group of Companies.

Library of Congress Cataloging-in-Publication Data

Chance, Jane. 1945–
The lord of the rings : the mythology of power / Jane Chance.
p. cm. — (Twayne's masterwork studies ; 99)
Includes bibliographical references and index.
ISBN 0-8057-9441-7 — ISBN 0-8057-8571-X (pbk.)
1. Tolkien, J. R. R. (John Ronald Reuel), 1892–1973. Lord of the rings. 2.
Fantastic fiction, English—History and criticism. 3. Power (Social sciences)
in literature. 4. Myth in literature. I. Title. II. Series: Twayne's
masterwork studies ; no. 99.
PR6039.032L6332 1992
823'.912—dc20   92-1402
                                           CIP

The paper used in this publication meets the minimum requirements of
American National Standard for Information Sciences Permanence of Paper
for Printed Library Materials, ANSI Z39.48-1984.

10 9 8 7 6 5 4 3 2 1 (alk. paper)

10 9 8 7 6 5 4 3 2 1 (pbk.: alk. paper)

Printed in the United States of America.

Contents

Note on the References and Acknowledgments

The edition of *The Lord of the Rings* used throughout is the three-volume standard second edition published in London by Allen & Unwin in 1966 and in Boston by Houghton Mifflin in 1967 (Ballantine Books reprinted a revised paper edition in 1965). References to *The Lord of the Rings* appear within parentheses and indicate volume and page numbers—*The Fellowship of the Ring* being volume 1; *The Two Towers*, 2; and *The Return of the King*, 3.

Quotations from the following works are reprinted by permission of Houghton Mifflin Co. *The Two Towers* by J. R. R. Tolkien. Text copyright © 1954 by George Allen & Unwin Ltd. Illustrations copyright © 1977 by The Folio Society Ltd. *The Return of the King* by J. R. R. Tolkien. Copyright © 1955, 1965 by J. R. R. Tolkien. Copyright © renewed 1983 by Christopher R. Tolkien, Michael H. R. Tolkien, John F. R. Tolkien, and Priscilla M. A. R. Tolkien. Copyright © 1965 by J. R. R. Tolkien. *The Fellowship of the Ring* by J. R. R. Tolkien. Copyright © 1965 by J. R. R. Tolkien.

Permission to quote from *The Fellowship of the Ring*, *The Two Towers*, and *The Return of the King* has been granted by HarperCollins. The illustration on p. 26, "The West Gate of Moria," is from *The Treason of Isengard* by J. R. R. Tolkien and is reproduced by kind permission of Unwin Hyman Ltd. Copyright © Unwin Hyman Ltd. The print is a reproduction of p. 3/3/10: llv of the J. R. R. Tolkien Manuscript Collection of the Marquette University Department of Special Collections and University Archives.

I wish to thank students in my freshman English "Heroic Quest" class at Rice University (fall 1989) for their patience in listening to my most recent ideas about Tolkien. The Dean of Humanities provided funds for a student, Lauren Phillips, to aid in collecting articles and checking documentation and also for an index. While writing his dissertation David Day collaborated with me on a review of medievalism in Tolkien studies, the fruits of which are in part reflected in the annotations to this volume's Bibliography. My research assistant, Kathye Bergen, rechecked the dates in the Chronology, the citations from Tolkien, and references; Larry Kraemer read over the copyedited manuscript and page proofs. Finally, my colleague Dr. Jill (Thad) Logan graciously read the manuscript and offered helpful suggestions for revision. To all of these persons I am indebted.

J. R. R. Tolkien in the study of his flat at 21 Merton Street, Oxford, September 1972. *Photograph © Billett Potter, Oxford*

Chronology: J. R. R. Tolkien's Life and Works

1892   John Ronald Reuel Tolkien is born in Bloemfontein, Orange Free State (South Africa), on 3 January.

1895   Along with his mother, Mabel, and his brother, Hilary (born 1894), moves to Birmingham, England, where his parents had lived before moving to South Africa.

1896   Tolkien's father, Arthur Reuel Tolkien, dies on 15 February and his family moves outside Birmingham to pastoral Sarehole. His mother begins his education in Latin, French, German, drawing, painting, and handwriting.

1900   Mabel Tolkien converts to Catholicism and introduces her sons to the faith; Tolkien enters King Edward VI School, and the family returns to Birmingham.

1903   Tolkien becomes a scholarship student at King Edward School and learns Greek and Middle English.

1904   Mabel Tolkien dies from diabetes complications on 14 November; Father Francis Morgan, a parish priest, becomes guardian for the Tolkien brothers and settles them at an aunt's.

1908   Unhappy there, the Tolkien boys are moved to Mrs. Faulkner's boardinghouse. At 16 Tolkien meets another lodger, the 19-year-old orphan Edith Bratt, his future wife.

1909   Tolkien and Edith fall in love; the Tolkien brothers are moved to a different lodging, and Edith moves away.

1910   Tolkien takes up debating at King Edward School—in Greek, Gothic, and Anglo-Saxon—and also learns some Old Norse and Spanish.

1911   Creates the Tea Club and Barrovian Society at grammar school, with friends Christopher Wiseman, R. Q. Wilson, and later Geoffrey B. Smith, an "ancestor" group of "the Inklings." On his second examination attempt is granted a scholarship to study classics at Oxford University, but he prefers comparative philology.

1914   Writes "The Voyage of Earendel the Evening Star," based on an Anglo-Saxon line from Cynewulf's *Christ*.

1914–1918   World War I.

1915   Wins First Class Honors in English language and literature (that is, Old and Middle English especially) from Oxford and joins the British army (the Lancashire Fusiliers) as a second lieutenant. Geoffrey Smith also serves in this division.

1916   Marries Edith Bratt on 22 March, leaves for France on 4 June, and participates in the Battle of the Somme. R. Q. Wilson dies; Tolkien is stricken with "trench fever," returning home on 8 November. Geoffrey Smith dies from a gangrenous injury.

1917   Earliest writing: *The Silmarillion* begins, specifically, "The Fall of Gondolin." His first son, John, is born.

1918   Accepts a position as a junior staff member of the *Oxford English Dictionary*.

1920   His second son, Michael, is born. Begins *The Father Christmas Letters*. Accepts a position as reader of English language at Leeds University.

1922   Publishes *A Middle English Vocabulary*.

1924   Is promoted to professor of English language at Leeds—the youngest ever to hold such a professorship there. His third son, Christopher, is born.

1925   Tolkien and E. V. Gordon publish their edition of *Sir Gawain and the Green Knight.* Moves from Leeds to Oxford, where he becomes Rawlinson and Bosworth Professor of Anglo-Saxon. Lives at 22 Northmore Road until 1930, when the Tolkiens move to 20 Northmore, their home for 16 years.

1926   C. S. Lewis, Tolkien's future friend and Inkling member, author of *The Allegory of Love,* the Narnia series, and the *Perelandra* science fiction trilogy, joins the faculty at Oxford by May. Lewis and other dons read Icelandic sagas at Coalbiter gatherings (*Kolbítar* in Icelandic), an informal reading club founded by Tolkien.

1929   Tolkien's daughter, Priscilla, is born.

1930s   "The Inklings" is founded as a literary society in 1931 by an undergraduate named Tangye Lean for the purpose of reading unpublished writings; Tolkien and Lewis attend meetings, along with Major Warren Lewis (C. S. Lewis's brother), R. E. Havard (a doctor), Owen Barfield (Lewis's lawyer friend), and Hugo Dyson. In 1939 Charles Williams (of Oxford University Press) joins. Sometime in the 1930s *Farmer Giles of Ham* is written.

1930–1931? Narrates stories to his children; writes these words on an examination booklet: "In a hole in the ground there lived a hobbit."

1932   Shows the nearly complete manuscript of *The Hobbit* to Lewis late in the year.

1936	A former student and family friend, Elaine Griffiths, mentions to George Allen & Unwin Publishers that Tolkien has written children's stories, and the unfinished manuscript of *The Hobbit* is requested; Tolkien completes the work by the first week in October. On 25 November delivers the first Sir Israel Gollancz Memorial Lecture, "Beowulf: The Monsters and the Critics," before the British Academy; the lecture is also published as an essay.
1937	*The Hobbit* is published on 21 September and sells out by Christmas; Allen & Unwin asks for more but rejects the manuscript of what is to become *The Silmarillion*. Tolkien begins to write *The Lord of the Rings* in December.
1938?	Selects the title of his trilogy about the time Chamberlain signs the Munich Pact with Hitler.
1938	The American edition of *The Hobbit* wins the *New York Herald Tribune* prize for the best juvenile book that year. Tolkien reads *Farmer Giles* to an undergraduate society.
1939	On 8 March delivers the Andrew Lang Lecture, "On Fairy-Stories," at St. Andrews University in Scotland. (Andrew Lang collected fairy stories.) In September World War II begins in Europe.
1943	Albert Hoffman in Switzerland discovers psychotic reactions to LSD (lysergic acid diethylamide), to be used for psychotherapeutic reasons in the 1940s and 1950s. Tolkien finishes book 3 of *Rings*.
1945	The war in Europe ends on 9 May; in August the atomic bomb is dropped on Hiroshima and Nagasaki. "Leaf by Niggle," an important short story by Tolkien, appears in print (it will be translated into Dutch, Swedish, French, German, and Japanese in the early 1970s). Tolkien becomes Merton Professor of English Language and Literature at Oxford University in the fall. His friendship with Lewis begins to cool.

1947	"On Fairy-Stories" is published (later to be translated into Swedish, Japanese, and Spanish). Tolkien shows *Rings* in manuscript to Rayner Unwin; continues to revise it.
1949	Publishes *Farmer Giles of Ham* (it will be translated into Swedish, Polish, German, Dutch, Hebrew, German, Italian, Japanese, and Spanish in the 1960s and 1970s).
1950	Much of *Rings* is complete, but Tolkien quarrels with Stanley Unwin, insisting that the firm also publish *The Silmarillion;* changes publishers.
1950–1953	Korean War.
1952	Tolkien returns to Allen & Unwin.
1954	*The Fellowship of the Ring* and *The Two Towers* are published.
1955	*The Return of the King* is published. Tolkien ceases to meet regularly with Lewis.
1956	*Rings* is translated into Dutch: during the next 20 years it will be translated into Swedish, Polish, Danish, German, Italian, French, Japanese, Finnish, Norwegian, and Portuguese.
1959	Retires from the Merton professorship.
1962	Publishes *The Adventures of Tom Bombadil*.
1963	C. S. Lewis dies on 22 November.
1964	Publishes *Tree and Leaf* ("Leaf by Niggle" plus "On Fairy-Stories").
1965	Ace Books, an American science fiction publisher, issues an unauthorized paperback edition of *Rings*. Ballantine Books later publishes the authorized edition, and Tolkien places pressure on Ace Books (through notes to American fans) to pay him royalties. Writes *Smith of Wootton Major*.
1965–1968	Hippies and the counterculture emerge in America. *Rings* sells 3 million copies in paperback.

1965–1975   Vietnam War.

1966   A collection of earlier stories and essays, *The Tolkien Reader*, is published in America.

1967   Publishes *Smith of Wootton Major*. Che Guevera is shot by the Bolivian army on 8 October.

1968   Rudi Dutschke, leader of Students for a Democratic Society, is shot in Berlin on Easter. In Paris Sorbonne students ally with Renault autoworkers and riot. In August student Yippies (short for Youth International party) demonstrate against the Vietnam War at the Democratic National Convention in Chicago. Students generally become interested in Marx, Engels, Lenin, and Marcuse. The Tolkiens move to Bournemouth, a seaside resort. *Poems and Songs of Middle-earth*, a record of Tolkien's poems in English and Elvish set to music, is issued.

1971   Edith dies on 29 November.

1972   In March Tolkien returns to Merton College at Oxford as resident honorary fellow. Receives an honorary doctorate of letters from Oxford and is made a Commander of the British Empire.

1973   Dies on 2 September from an acute bleeding gastric ulcer and chest infection. Is buried in Oxford (with Edith).

1976   *The Father Christmas Letters* is published with the aid of daughter-in-law Baillie Tolkien.

1977   *The Silmarillion* is published with the aid of Christopher; Tolkien's biography appears in print.

1980   *Unfinished Tales* is published with the aid of Christopher.

1981   An edition of Tolkien's *Letters* is published with the aid of Christopher.

LITERARY AND
HISTORICAL CONTEXT

✛

1

Tolkien's World: A Voice
for the Dispossessed

J. R. R. Tolkien, medieval scholar and storyteller, was nevertheless a modern man whose life and writings reflect the stresses and dysfunctions of the twentieth-century world. Born in South Africa in 1892, he was moved at the age of three to a town near Birmingham in England. This traumatic journey existentially shaped much of his early perception of reality: "Quite by accident, I have a very vivid child's view, which was the result of being taken away from one country and put in another hemisphere—the place where I belonged but which was totally novel and strange. After the barren, arid heat a Christmas tree. But no, it was not an unhappy childhood. It was full of tragedies but it didn't tot up to an unhappy childhood."[1] These "tragedies" refer to his home life. He lost his father the year after the move from South Africa, when he was 4; at the age of 12 (1904) he also lost his mother.

It is perhaps no accident that for security Tolkien turned inward, and to school and schooling. Taught by his Catholic mother until he won a scholarship to grammar school, he became adept enough at his studies also to win a scholarship to study classics at Oxford (1911). Because of his success in medieval English languages and comparative philology, however, he changed his course of study, which resulted in First Class Honors at graduation. And he remained more or less attached to a university for the rest of his life—after a brief interruption by World War I and a foray into the British army in 1915, when he was wounded, returned to England,

and married another orphan, three years his senior, in 1916.

Tolkien's career thereafter reflected two significant influences. The first was language, naming, perceived as a philosophical means of ordering reality, which catalyzed Tolkien's interest in classical and medieval languages. His first creative writing of any note, *The Silmarillion*, was intended originally as the history of an invented world to represent his created languages but was never completed during his lifetime. His interest in language led him first to join the staff of *The Oxford English Dictionary* (1918) and later to become a reader of English language at Leeds University (1920), Rawlinson and Bosworth Professor of Anglo-Saxon at Oxford (1925), and Merton Professor of English Language and Literature at Oxford (1945).

Tolkien's love of language, and thus his love of medieval language, pervades his fictional writing. He delivered his groundbreaking scholarly lecture on "Beowulf: The Monsters and the Critics" a year before he published *The Hobbit* (1937), and clearly his understanding of the Anglo-Saxon poem colored his creation of this "children's story."

A second significant influence on Tolkien's career were the omnipresent physical and spiritual threats to security—within the family, within society, within his nation—whenever war intervened, as World Wars I and II did during Tolkien's lifetime. These historical events catalyzed and shaped his writing. World War I interrupted his peaceful studies at the university; he joined the army in 1915 and married Edith Bratt in 1916, the same year in which he came down with trench fever during the Battle of the Somme, a malaise that forced him to retire. The year he began writing *The Silmarillion* (1917) his first son was born. In 1937 he published *The Hobbit*; he claims to have started *The Lord of the Rings* during Hitler's rise to power. The trilogy was actually published in 1954 and 1955. Tolkien notes in his foreword that

> this tale grew in the telling, until it became a history of the Great War of the Ring and included many glimpses of the yet more ancient history that preceded it. . . . [T]he composition of *The Lord of the Rings* went on at intervals during the years 1936 to 1949, a period in which I had many duties that I did not neglect, and many other interests as a learner and teacher that often absorbed me. The delay was, of course, also increased by the outbreak of war in 1939, by the end of which year the tale had not yet reached the end of Book I. In spite of the darkness of the next five

4

years, I found that the story could not now be wholly abandoned, and I plodded on, mostly by night, till I stood at Balin's tomb in Moria. There I halted for a long while. It was almost a year later when I went on and so came to Lothlórien and the Great River late in 1941. In the next year I wrote the first drafts of the matter that now stands as Book III, and the beginnings of Chapters 1 and 3 of Book V; and there, as the beacons flared in Anórien and Théoden came to Harrowdale, I stopped. . . .

It was during 1944 that, leaving the loose ends and perplexities of a war which it was my task to conduct, or at least to report, I forced myself to tackle the journey of Frodo to Mordor. These chapters, eventually to become Book IV, were written and sent out as a serial to my son, Christopher, then in South Africa with the R.A.F. Nonetheless it took another five years before the tale was brought to its present end. (1: viii, ix)

Even during the time *Rings* became popular among college students and young people throughout the world—that is, during the Korean and Vietnam wars—a war of one kind or another provided a backdrop for the imagination, whether of author or reader.

For the author the devastation and rebuilding of Europe occurred during this long period of writing and revision, and the audience of his children—for Tolkien had begun telling tales when his children were very young, to which *The Hobbit* and *The Father Christmas Letters* testify—continued to provide a "readership" for him throughout this long span. One can imagine Tolkien's parental concern for Christopher, who was a member of the Royal Air Force stationed abroad during World War II, fueling his epistolary serialization of book 4, the second half of *The Two Towers*. The reader is not only a child but an heir, Tolkien's future, and like Gandalf to Bilbo, or Bilbo to Frodo, Tolkien wanted to promise a better world for his own progeny. Tolkien indeed noted that "children aren't a class. They are merely human beings at different stages of maturity. All of them have a human intelligence which even at its lowest is a pretty wonderful thing, and the entire world is in front of them" (Norman, 100).

Perhaps because Tolkien recognized the specialness of such marginalized or disempowered groups as hobbits, children, and college students, *Rings* was received enthusiastically. It is no accident that the paperback version sold 3 million copies between 1965 and 1968: its success coincided with the worldwide student demonstrations of the late 1960s that were centered in Paris and

Chicago and encompassed university sit-ins to protest the draft, patriarchal control of education that seemed "irrelevant," and students' lack of a voice in their own educations or lives. At that time students perceived big business as the force dominating political decisions (which meant the Vietnam War and therefore their own lives, if they would be drafted to serve and possibly to die) and viewed the CIA as an underground organization infiltrating and toppling foreign governments; students' mistrust of government was paramount. John F. Kennedy and Lyndon B. Johnson were Democratic American presidents whose victory seemed to guarantee support of and by the people. Hippies and the underground drug cult, powered by a renaissance in rock music intended for drug consumption (chiefly marijuana, hashish, LSD, and magic mushrooms), urged a vision of peace, love, brotherhood, communal life, and hallucinogenic and surreal fantasies otherworldly in nature. It was the right time for a cult work like *Rings*—indeed, the *Harvard Lampoon* published a bawdy and psychedelic parody in 1969 entitled *Bored of the Rings*.

The historical context for Tolkien's writing of *Rings* and for its reception thus reveals a world in turmoil and chaos. World War I had shattered the perception of European civilization as an oasis from bloodshed—Tolkien himself lost two of his three dearest boyhood friends in that war.[2] The Germans first used chlorine gas at the Battle of Ypres; the Lusitania was sunk; and the Russian war effort collapsed. World War II, for Great Britain, brought home closer still the imminence of invasion because of the devastation brought about by air raids. In 1946 U-boats blockaded Britain. In the decade or so after World War II there began the long cold war, whose tensions between East and West were exacerbated by the creation of the atomic bomb and the threat of nuclear war.[3] The Korean War in the 1950s in which the United States found itself involved was followed by the Vietnam War of the mid 1960s and early 1970s. It is no wonder that Tolkien provided a voice for the dispossessed in what was initially viewed only as an eccentric but popular work of fantasy—*The Lord of the Rings*.

2

The Importance of the Work

The importance of J. R. R. Tolkien as a scholar of Old and Middle English language and literature had been recognized by his peers in England long before *Rings* was published. In 1936—the year before *The Hobbit* was published—Tolkien delivered before the British Academy the first Sir Israel Gollancz Memorial Lecture; entitled "Beowulf: The Monsters and the Critics," his lecture was to become an influential essay. In it he argued for the treatment of *Beowulf* as a great poem instead of as a text for the study of anthropology, philology, and history. Appearing at the same time as the rise of New Criticism, which similarly studied the text as text, without recourse to external contexts or materials, the essay received wide scholarly acclaim and changed the direction of the reading of *Beowulf*. In addition, Tolkien's joint critical edition (with E. V. Gordon) of *Sir Gawain and the Green Knight* spurred modern study of the *Gawain*-Poet. Tolkien's work on *The Oxford English Dictionary*, a fact little recognized today, contributed to its phenomenal range and influenced his own work on the languages of Middle-earth. He married philology to literary criticism in a happy union of normally opposed approaches.

But it was the 1937 publication of *The Hobbit* that revealed Tolkien's power as a storyteller in both England and America: a story originally intended for children came to have widespread appeal to a larger audience. Because of the popularity of that work, Tolkien's publisher, Allen & Unwin, asked him for "more about Hobbits." The result—a 1,200-page, three-volume novel with two books in each volume, entitled *The Lord of the Rings* and first appearing in print in 1954–55—occasioned widespread popularity, unauthorized paperback publication in the United States, and a Tolkien cult of millions, especially in the 1960s and early 1970s. The fantasy was translated into more than 10 languages, from Dutch to Japanese.

The popularity of the work coincided with a contemporary need for escape from the political and military tensions wracking the world and for stability in an increasingly unstable environment. A much-copied graffito of the antiestablishment 1960s acknowledged that "God is dead," but the acknowledgment was glossed by its inversion in the equally popular graffito that "Frodo lives." Frodo, the central hobbit hero who had retired among the elves at the end of *Rings*, like the omnipresent and immortal Arthur of the Welsh legends whose intention to return to power was inscribed in Thomas Malory's medieval romance, epitomized the popular need for lasting values at a time of the Vietnam War. Accordingly, for college students and others the U.S. government took on the guise of a Dark Lord demanding universal domination in tiny countries of little interest to most Americans and the submission of Americans' individual rights and beliefs to the national demand for more combat troops in an alien country.

Rings today, as the subject of hundreds of critical and scholarly books, essays, dissertations, theses, and journals, has finally been accepted as the masterpiece that it is. There are more than 10 essay collections dealing with Tolkien's life and work, as well as a biography and collection of his letters. His lesser works about Middle-earth, *The Silmarillion* and *The Unfinished Tales*, are perceived as important for setting forth philological, legendary, and mythological blueprints for the world he created. They also thus provide a significant philosophical and moral context for the greater work. The remnants of all Tolkien's unfinished writings have been edited and published by his son Christopher, who has placed them chronologically according to the order of their writing.

The genius of the "three-decker novel" (as its author termed it) transcends his creation of a whole fantastic or "secondary" world of "sub-creation" (to use Tolkien's terminology in his essay "On Fairy-Stories")[4] with 14 invented languages (including the most complete, Quenya, or the elven tongue), each obedient to its own internal laws. In some ways a mirror image of the pastoral England that

Tolkien and the other "Inklings" (Tolkien's circle of friends who met to read their manuscripts) idealized in opposition to the rise of late-Victorian urban industrialization, the Shire within Middle-earth seemed to guarantee a near-utopian existence for its childlike hobbit inhabitants—a group to which a part of us all, regardless of generation, nation, and age, desires to belong.

In addition, *Rings* has been generally recognized as a powerful work of creative imagination whose levels of understanding are dependent on the synthesis and assimilation of a variety of medieval and modern materials. The masterpiece offers a twentieth-century understanding of the nature of good and evil, the value of community, the natural order of the universe, and the singularity of the individual. In this modern age with which mechanization and the totalitarianism of Big Brother are popularly associated, freedom may seem to have counted for little. Against this backdrop Tolkien sets his narrative, an age in which the individual appears powerless against fate and the universal horror of evil, whether in Auschwitz and Eastern Europe, South Africa, or southern California.

The critical reputation of *Rings* continues to undergo revision and amplification, as does its historical role in English literature. A mere four decades after its publication, *Rings* has already assumed its place as a long, heroic epic-romance on the shelf next to the works of Spenser and Malory. In his introduction to a collection of essays on Tolkien, editor Robert Giddings noted that "all texts signify, but not all texts are significant. It seems to me that insofar as *The Lord of the Rings* shapes, textures and conditions the nature of our perceptions of the world we live in, insofar as it is used in negotiating the construction of our realities, then it is extremely significant" (Giddings, 18–19). As a modern work, *Rings* might then be studied as part of the literary movement in the 1930s to the 1950s in which T. S. Eliot, Evelyn Waugh, and Graham Greene, among others, either turned to or fled from Catholicism and religious faith.

Tolkien has also been described as a mythographer equal in stature to the Puritan poet John Milton and, even more especially, the Romantic poet William Blake. Furthermore, as philologists and linguists are just now realizing, Tolkien's brilliance in language creation and analysis reveals far more about his role as a philosopher of language. We might add, at this moment, that as a theory of power his fiction offers complex solutions to contemporary political, economic, and ideological theoretical problems voiced by Michel Foucault and other thinkers—Tolkien's contemporaries in the 1960s and 1970s.

The importance of Tolkien's *The Lord of the Rings* has indeed evolved since its inception.

3

Critical Reception

Although the separate volumes of *Rings* were published in hard-cover in 1954 and 1955, the trilogy did not become a best-seller until 1966, when it was issued as a paperback by Ballantine Books and quickly attained the number-one spot. Apparently its unauthorized paperback publication the year before by Ace Books (a science fiction publisher) in part stimulated two science fiction/fantasy editors at Ballantine Books to publish the trilogy as a Christmas boxed set for $2.85. The initial 50,000 copies sold out, and word about it spread among college students, who made *Rings* into a cult book. Unfortunately, this same cult celebration delayed Tolkien's entry into the canon of twentieth-century writers within the academy, which has always mistrusted the appeal of the popular.

In regard to its literary value, the earliest reviews of *The Fellowship of the Ring* (1954) and *The Two Towers* (1954, 1955) were decidedly mixed. Reviewers in the small English book reviews praised *Fellowship* for its serious purpose, imaginative writing, and rich fantasy. It was termed an "extraordinary" book that cannot be classified, one of the "most significant literary achievements of modern times." Others, however, found it "pretentious snobbery," a "scholarly off-shoot of a once-done fairy tale," a "long pedestrian fairy-story for adults," an "enchanting freak," "tedious," "repetitious," and "boring."[5]

Famous names and well-known journals reviewed the early volumes with equally mixed results. Tolkien's friend C. S. Lewis termed it a victory as romance, a whole world, myth without allegory.[6] In contrast, the eminent critic Edwin Muir noted that

Tolkien's characters are either good or evil, never both: "And if Mr. Tolkien's imagination had been equal to his invention, and his style equal to both, this book might have been a masterpiece."[7] In the United States Orville Prescott criticized Tolkien's superficial characterization and acknowledged the work's failure: Tolkien as a writer of romantic fantasy fails in comparison with E. R. Eddison.[8] It is worth noting, however, that Chaucer critic Edward Wagenknecht perhaps sensed *Fellowship*'s future importance and termed it "a great work of the imagination . . . wonderful as story alone and the prose a consistent glory" and in a second review praised this "prose romance" and also its author for creating, Blake-like, his own mythology.[9]

Towers received perhaps less attention: the *New Yorker* noted that "Mr. Tolkien writes with love and precision, but . . . he is tedious a good deal of the time."[10] Most of the reviews appeared in science fiction journals and local newspapers, although the *Times Literary Supplement* read this "prose epic in praise of courage" so that "Westernesse . . . comes to rank in the reader's imagination with Asgard and Camelot."[11]

Early newspaper reviewers, as well as later scholars and critics, were puzzled from the first about the exact formal and generic categories to which Tolkien's work belonged. Whether it was epic, romance, fantasy, or fairy tale, most agreed it was a work of imagination, creating its own mythology; embodying such moral values as nobility, courage, loyalty, and truth; and deriving from the Norse sagas, Old English heroic poems, and medieval romances. Charles A. Brady attempted to pinpoint the diminutive genius of *Towers* by saying, "It scales down to the dimensions of the story the most tremendous and immutable moral truths. . . . *The Two Towers* is a nursery Nibelungenlied, a domesticated Inferno, a Paradise Lost diminished for the fireside consideration of Robin Goodfellow."[12] The great names against which his achievement was measured define Tolkien's literary context—Spenser, Ariosto, Malory, Carroll—as well as the great writers of children's literature and fairy tale—the Brothers Grimm, the authors of *The Wind in the Willows* and *The Sword in the Stone*—and the minor fantasists like John Cowper Powys in *Atlantis*, Fletcher Pratt in *Well of the Unicorn*, Poul Anderson in *The Broken Sword*, and E. R. Eddison.

Some of the early reviewers even acknowledged the relevance of

Rings for modern times: "The closeness of its analogy to the human situation gives it a dreadful reality and relevance. It is a prose-poet's rendering of the mental twilight of the modern world, darkened as it is by the black power . . . of the atom bomb." [13] Its "remarkable realism" renders it "terribly modern," other reviewers declared of *Fellowship*.

When literary critics came to analyze Tolkien's epic-romance, in the late 1950s and 1960s, they were mostly concerned about piecing together the thematic and imagistic paradigms on which the novel depends, or in defining the romance structure it shared with the romances of Charles Williams and C. S. Lewis—other members of the Inklings—or even boldly and elegantly treating it as real literature. [14] Several fanzines cropped up (*Mythlore, Tolkien Journal*); inexpensive guides for general readers and students—essentially plot summaries—came into print as paperbacks.

As the remainder of Tolkien's writings were published, in the 1970s and early 1980s, and a full-length bibliography was compiled (1970) and updated (1981), it became clear that Tolkien was not just a popular cult figure, an idol of the hippies and Yippies. More scholarly treatments emerged, along with the posthumous publication (by his son Christopher) of the uncompleted *Silmarillion* and *Unfinished Tales* and (by Humphrey Carpenter) of his *Letters* and an authorized biography. This legitimizing of Tolkien took several forms—book-length studies of the themes, imagery, symbolism, and psychology of the work and its relation to his other, more minor fictional pieces (Kocher, 1973, and Helms, 1974), in addition to a series of collected essays by several eminent university presses and independent small specialty presses.

Significantly affecting the academy's estimation of Tolkien has been medieval scholars' realization of both the importance of medievalism in Tolkien's fiction and the catalytic influence of philology on the languages he invented in his fiction. Carpenter convincingly made the connection in his 1977 biography: the primary link between medieval language and literature and Tolkien's creative transmogrification of both is two lines from the Old English Cynewulfian poem *Crist*, "Eala earendel, engla beorhtast, / ofer middangeard monnum sended" ("Hail Earendel, brightest of angels / above the Middle-earth sent to men"). [15] When Tolkien read these lines at Oxford University in 1914, he wrote, "I felt a curious thrill, as if something had stirred in me, half awakened from sleep. There was something very remote and strange and beautiful behind those words, as if I could grasp it, far beyond ancient English" (Carpenter, 64). As he studied Old Norse, the language of Iceland introduced by Norwegians fleeing their own country in the ninth century, Tolkien was impelled to compose a poem spurred by those Old English lines. It was his first creation, entitled "The Voyage of Earendel the Evening Star," and it began,

> Earendel sprang up from the Ocean's cup
> In the gloom of the mid-world's rim,
> From the door of Night as a ray of light
> Leapt over the twilight brim,
> And launching his bark like a silver spark
> From the golden fading sand
> Down the sunlit breath of Day's fiery death
> He sped from Westerland.
>
> (Carpenter, 71)

In 1915 this poem grew further, into the "Lay of Earendel," which described the encounter of the voyaging Earendel with the elves that Tolkien imagined as speaking a fairy language heavily influenced by Finnish. This poem, this invented language, carried the seeds for the mythology of Middle-earth that would bloom in *The Silmarillion* and later in *Rings*. Once established, this pattern—medieval language and literary work triggering Tolkien's linguistic imagination and literary aesthetic—continued to influence his creative production.

In support of Carpenter's insight, a festschrift was published in 1979 (six years after Tolkien's death) by a university press and edited by two medievalists, Tolkien's former student Mary Salu and Anglo-Saxon scholar Robert T. Farrell. In this volume such medieval scholars as Derek Brewer and Thomas H. Shippey analyze the medieval underpinnings of his literary work and created languages. My own study, *Tolkien's Art: "A Mythology for England,"* also appeared in 1979; it relates the themes and images of Tolkien's minor works to his major works and explores both for signs of his scholarship on Old and Middle English literature. Among the most significant in influencing his own evolving works were the Old and Middle English works he loved best (as reflected in the criticism he wrote about them)—works such as *Beowulf, The Battle of Maldon, Ancrene Riwle, Sir Gawain and the Green Knight, Pearl,* and Chaucer's *fabliaux.* Also influential were Tolkien's own essays on the works and his earliest fictionizations of those essays—"Beowulf: The Monsters and the Critics," "The Homecoming of Beorhtnoth Beorhthelm's Son," and *The Hobbit.* All became grist for Tolkien's fine medievalistic mill.

Related and more specific studies of Tolkien's medievalism have primarily acknowledged the impact on his epic-romance of names, setting and landscape, beings, characters, genres, and even philosophical systems.[16] For his names Tolkien drew on Old and Middle High German, Icelandic, Dutch, Swedish, Old Norse, the Celtic languages, and Latin, as he acknowledged in the guide for translators compiled after the Swedish and Dutch translations were published.[17] Apparently he also derived some names from Greek and Hebrew and from Old English.[18] In most cases the name of a character, species, weapon, or place had an etymological appropriateness that revealed some hidden or inner reality (e.g., "Mordor," from the Old English word for murder and death). Basically Old English, Old Norse, and Celtic most influenced the creation of his own Middle-earth languages, including Rohirric, Dwarvish, Quenya (or High-elvish), and Sindarin (or Common Elvish).[19] From the *Eddas* come the names of dwarves; the names of Gandalf, the Ring, the dwarves, and the elves are borrowed from Scandinavian myth.[20] From Old English words come important concepts and types: the loyal subordinate is drawn from the *heorothwerod,* the band of retainers supporting the chief.[21]

In his theory of fantasy and the construction of a secondary world in the three-decker novel, Tolkien also inherited ideas about recovery and subcreation, the secondary world, from earlier models. For creating his setting Tolkien extricated from Norse and Celtic mythology various images and landscapes, including the trees, Yggdrasill, the sacred groves of Norse community ritual life, and the Undying Lands, from the Celtic Immortal Isles.[22] Species of Middle-earth in particular were shaped by Northern saga—the hobbits, elves, orcs, dwarves, wizards, and men of Gondor (Norse men).[23] His characters were deeply influenced by medieval and Renaissance models, among them the fairy-tale hero (Frodo), the epic hero and the healing king (Aragorn), the loyal retainer Wiglaf and Bedivere

(Sam Gamgee),[24] and the Grendel-like monster in *Beowulf* (Gollum, originating in *The Hobbit*).[25] Tolkien also combines W. H. Auden's two types of hero (possibly in Frodo and Aragorn), the valorous and exceptional epic hero and the modest fairy-tale hero, the latter Christianized by Tolkien.[26]

The narrative structure of *Rings* and its genre may also have been influenced by its classical and medieval antecedents. As an epic *Rings* chiefly mirrors Virgil's *Aeneid* and perhaps *Beowulf*, in its emphasis on battle; such heroic qualities as loyalty and valor, wisdom and fortitude; and the obligatory descent into the under-world (as represented by Mordor).[27] As a saga it resembles the Norse-Icelandic *Eddas* and sagas and the *Kalevala*,[28] but its loosely episodic technique of branching journey-quests most approximates *entrelacement*, a medieval romance characteristic.[29] Symbolism, the idea of quest and its accompanying themes of search and transition, an atmosphere of death and disaster, and the growth and development of a young hero are other romance characteristics.[30] Chief among the specific models identified are Sir Gawain (from *Sir Gawain and the Green Knight*), for Frodo's loss of innocence and self-discovery,[31] and Perceval (the hero both of Chrétien de Troyes and also Wolfram von Eschenbach), in the ro-mance of the same name, for the moral quality of the quest and its religious seeking.[32] Of prime interest in comparing Tolkien's ro-mance with earlier models is his inversion of the norm: Frodo must give up his quest at the end, and he in fact does not succeed; Gol-lum as adversary both subverts and achieves the quest; the heroes battle death peacefully.[33] Finally, the medieval genre of the dream vision has been identified as a source in relation to at least one fig-ure: John Gower's *Confessio Amantis* and the allegorical priest Ge-nius (who absolves the lover Amans from his courtly love sins) as the conscience of Nature parallels Tom Bombadil in *Fellowship*.[34]

In using these early sources Tolkien has been recognized as a master assimilator: for example, he synthesizes the Germanic pa-gan concept of *lif is laene*, life is loaned, implying the necessity of a return of that loan, and the Christian concept of submission to God's will.[35] In addition, however, his use of Latin (late antique and early medieval) sources for the philosophy of *Rings* and what in other hands might be termed "moral allegory" has also been identi-fied. From Boethius's sixth-century and heavily influential *Consola-*

tion of Philosophy Tolkien may have borrowed the reconciliation of Providence, fate, and free will that helps to explain the often-antithetical statements in the novel about chance and fate.[36] Indebted to Platonic and Neoplatonic philosophy are his theory of naming and the concept of equivocal reality that it reflects, as well as his Augustinian concept of evil as privation.[37] Prudentius's fourth-century *Psychomachia*, with its battle between virtues and vices, may have influenced the dramatic battle between Sam and Frodo and the spider Shelob.[38] Finally, the novel is deeply governed by the idea of *discordia concors*, the medieval and Renaissance concept of everything in its place, order emerging out of disorder.[39]

Thus from the late 1960s into the 1990s the fiction-writing Tolkien's academic reputation has been ensured. *Seven*, a scholarly journal devoted to the Inklings, appeared in 1980, and scholarly articles revealing the complex medieval philological and literary seams of Tolkien's fictive fabric have been published in such journals as *Names, Anglia, Twentieth-Century Literature, Word,* and *Mosaic*. The publication of *The Silmarillion* (1977) had disclosed Tolkien's role as a philosopher of language and demanded that the reader attend to the Middle-earth chronology of his canon—*The Silmarillion* first, *The Hobbit* second, and then *Rings*—so that *Rings* is read with the complex mythology of the far-older work in mind. The work of critics like Verlyn Flieger[40] and David Lyle Jeffrey[41] demonstrates Tolkien's hitherto-ignored position as a philosopher of language and points to new paths in Tolkien criticism worthy of further investigation. Master's theses and doctoral dissertations continue to appear; handbooks and concordances aiding the scholarly reading of Tolkien have been added to the bookshelf, among them two studies by Ruth Noel, one on the mythological background of Tolkien's writing (*The Mythology of Middle-earth*, 1977) and the other a detailed grammar of his created languages, especially Quenya (*The Languages of Tolkien's Middle-earth*, 1980).[42] A 1971 encyclopedia of terms and names in Tolkien's Middle-earth—an aid to the general reader and student—was enlarged and updated in 1978 by Robert Foster.[43] The direction of recent scholarly articles has been to the genius of those created languages as a means of discerning the nature of the created species who speak them and thereby interpreting Tolkien's fictive masterpiece. Another direction is toward interdisciplinary studies of

4

Power and Knowledge in Tolkien

Tolkien shares with the social philosopher and theorist Michel Foucault similar concerns relating to the question of power and knowledge. Although Tolkien's major fiction did not emerge in response to the political and academic events in France during the late 1960s, as did Foucault's, he nevertheless spent most of his mature life as a professor working within the British equivalent of the academy, and his greatest popularity coincided with the same historical phenomenon—the rise of student power during the late 1960s and early 1970s. To provide this context for the study of Tolkien, then, is to invite comparison with a thinker whose views on the question of power and knowledge are remarkably similar.

Most important, both thinkers question power as sovereignty, power as substance. "Power in the substantive sense, 'le' pouvoir, doesn't exist," notes Foucault. "In reality power means relations, a more-or-less organised, hierarchical, co-ordinated cluster of relations."[45] This concept of a power grid implies constant change and flux and therefore by definition a "complex domain" (Foucault, 188) of particular powers and many issues. To analyze this network we must look at the whole interworking rather than the responsibility of the individual alone—that is, we must look at what might be termed the domain of the political: "Every relation of force implies at each moment a relation of power (which is in a sense its momentary expression) and every power relation makes a reference, as its effect but also as its condition of possibility, to a political field of which it forms a part" (Foucault, 189). Tolkien, as we shall see, might well agree with this politicization of power—and knowledge.

Like Foucault, both Tolkien and his fellow Inkling C. S. Lewis questioned the validity of the human sciences to represent the rationality of the age. Foucault focused on the institutional matrices of hospital and asylum at a time when the working class was in revolt against the power of institutions, whether schools, hospitals, or prisons, and therefore against the knowledge they claimed as their province. Tolkien fictionalized this institutional matrix through the creation of the Dark Lord Sauron and his imitators linked with the land of death, Mordor, that he ruled so tyrannously. All three thinkers object to the deployment of post-Enlightenment technologies in the governance of peoples.

In "The Eye of Power" Foucault defines the essential institutional model as Bentham's eighteenth-century architectural device of the "Panopticon," a ring-shaped building enclosing a tower that oversees cells that might contain a convict—or a lunatic, a patient, a worker, or a student (Foucault, 147). It is the same model used by Tolkien to locate the nature of Sauron's power, Saruman's power, Shelob's power, and even the Sackville-Bagginses' power. Visibility—the searching Eye of Sauron—is necessary to ensure access to all individuals; it is this same visibility that insists on a rigorous and universal power. The ultimate form of visibility locates within the individual, or what Foucault describes as "the gaze"—"an inspecting gaze, a gaze which each individual under its weight will end by interiorising to the point that he is his own overseer, each individual thus exercising this surveillance over, and against, himself. A superb formula: power exercised continuously and for what turns out to be a minimal cost. When Bentham realizes what he has discovered, he calls it the Colombus's egg of political thought, a formula exactly the opposite of monarchical power" (Foucault, 155). Through this structure power becomes a "machinery that no one owns" (Foucault, 156). For this reason there is no point in the prisoners taking over the tower in Bentham's Panopticon: in echo of one of Frodo's central points about "ownership" of the Ring (a type of Panopticon), Foucault asks rhetorically, "Do you think it would be much better to have the prisoners operating the Panoptic apparatus and sitting in the central tower, instead of the guards?" (Foucault, 164–65).

Like Tolkien, Foucault has criticized the concept of power as formulated through the repressive speech act of the "interdict," or the "enunciation of law, discourse of prohibition" (Foucault, 140). Instead, Foucault has identified a positive desire for productive power running through the social body (Foucault, 119), necessitating the "incorporation" of power in order to gain access to individuals' bodies (Foucault, 125). And it is the intellectual ("the clear, individual figure of a universality whose obscure, collective form is embodied in the proletariat" [Foucault, 126]), especially within the university, who has become most aware of specific struggles in the precise arenas that work or life has engaged him or her. J. Robert Oppenheimer is a good example of the post–World War II "specific" intellectual: this one individual possessed the scientific knowledge to make the atomic bomb, whose destructive capability posed a "universal" political threat (Foucault, 128). If we substitute "Saruman," "Gandalf," or even "Bilbo" and "Frodo" for Oppenheimer, we begin to understand how Tolkien's concept of the wizard, or the scholar-historian who bears the Ring, functions analogously to the figure of the specific intellectual embodying the "proletariat." Like Foucault, Tolkien is concerned with the political problem of the intellectual, one not of "science" or "ideology" but of "truth" and "power." And so Foucault concludes his essay "Truth and Power" by stating, "It's not a matter of emancipating truth from every system of power (which would be a chimera, for truth is already power) but of detaching the power of truth from the forms of hegemony, social, economic and cultural, within which it operates at the present time. . . . The political question, to sum up, is not error, illusion, alienated consciousness, or ideology; it is truth itself" (Foucault, 133).

The power of truth and its liberation from hegemony are indeed the great themes of *Rings*. A novel that mythologizes power and the problem of individual difference (as theoretically defined), *Rings* in its three volumes focuses on the problem of individual and class difference within the social body or construct (*Fellowship*), the heroic power of knowledge and language in the political power struggle (*Towers*), and the ideal of kingship as healing and service, in a unique inversion of master-servant roles and the domination of one by the other (*Return*).

The introduction to this mythology of power begins with the role of the individual within society as symbolized by "The Birthday Party," the first and most important chapter of *Fellowship* and thus of *Rings*. Here this conventional celebration of the individual, the self (Bilbo in this case), is marked by his gift-giving to others (liberality) and climaxes in his disappearance. Intellectual heroism, in Tolkien's world, is achieved through social involvement, service to others, and the disappearance of self-indulgence. The "gift" of the Ring by Bilbo to his nephew Frodo is the gift of invisibility, because wearing it "stretches" the self: that is, resisting the desire to submit to the authority of its maker, Sauron, wears out any individual, but over time this resistance paradoxically strengthens the determination to resist.

In succeeding chapters of this study, the individual is seen to use this gift to test resistance to institutionalized power and the power of others within the community. In *Fellowship* language as the articulation of knowledge and desire serves as moral and political weaponry against threats to survival and community (which often take the form of subversive language and its concomitant power). In *Towers* knowledge, as reflected in the power of language, can be used or misused as an effective and manipulative weapon by the powerful, or those who aspire to power—Wormtongue and Saruman, chiefly. The adversaries in *Towers* also include the inarticulate and dumb (Gollum, Shelob) whose rage leads to murder, or Mordor: a greater evil than the cunning manipulation of words is wordless and mindless violence, untamable by communication or rational discourse.

But this second volume also reveals the civilizing power of service to others—Gollum, serving Master Frodo, becomes Sméagol. Similarly, in the third volume, *Return*, the leader's true power emerges from wise and healing service to the community. The maintenance of society is best advanced by the caretaker and the gardener, those who nurture others and continue the work of the family or nation. In their role of understanding and tolerating individual differences within the community—indeed, using those differences productively—the caretakers empower both the individual and society, or, together, the social network.

The context, then, from which Tolkien derives his vision of power is institutional and political, like that of Foucault—the university, academia. And the philosophy Tolkien propounds is accordingly constructed with the tools of the specific intellectual—the power of language in attaining the primary goal—the pursuit of truth. Both the context and the philosophy are concealed by the veil of the heroic narrative, whose singular structure, repeated in its various books, assumes a power of its own.

A READING

✥

This drawing by Tolkien (from *The Treason of Isengard*) shows the West Gate to the Mines of Moria. Reproduced by permission of Unwin Hyman Ltd.

5

The Problem of Difference
in "The Birthday Party"

It is not altogether clear from reading *Fellowship* and *Rings* the first time (much less the fifth or the tenth) how politically aware and involved the hobbits Bilbo and his nephew Frodo are, even in the introductory chapter, "The Birthday Party." This lack of clarity arises because the Shire in which they live exudes a pastoral innocence that masks the seeds of its potential destruction. We recall the "charming, absurd, helpless hobbits" (1: 79) in the Shire, whom Gandalf worries might become enslaved by Sauron, the "kind, jolly, stupid Bolgers, Hornblowers, Boffins, Bracegirdles . . . . not to mention the ridiculous Bagginses" (1: 79). For the moment they are protected because Sauron has "more useful" servants, but there is always a threat from him because of his "malice and revenge." And yet the difference between the isolated, safe, jolly Shire and the distant, evil Dark Power is not as marked as it might seem, for there exist power struggles among the different hobbit species (families) in the Shire region, absurd in some cases and significant in others. One mark of the ability of Bilbo and Frodo—their power—is their sensitivity to the politics of the Shire, a faculty born of nurture and nature that will facilitate Frodo's mission and attract followers.

The political problems in the Shire grow out of its deceptively "safe" isolation from the rest of Middle-earth. Its inhabitants distrust those who come from outside, who are different from them in ways they do not understand. A stranger—initially and more familiarly a Brandybuck; later and more ominously a Dark Rider—arouses mistrust, and the inhabitants band closer together. Sandyman the Miller from the beginning creates a problem for Frodo through his suspicious notice of the queerness of the visitors to Bag End (among whom are the strange dwarves and the magical Gandalf). This queerness therefore extends also to Bag End itself and ultimately, by association, to its owners, Bilbo and then Frodo (1: 47). Sameness is familiar and secure, and sameness means hobbitlike. The hobbits relish what is natural for them, which involves physical activities, living close to nature—dwelling in holes, eating, smoking tobacco. To do otherwise is unhobbitlike. "Hobbits," Tolkien once acknowledged, "have what you might call universal morals. I should say they are examples of natural philosophy and natural religion."[46] Marks of distinction—wealth, education, even leadership—can set a hobbit apart, make him different. The major political problem for any potential leader, then, is to maintain the trust of those led—to make leadership seem "natural" and to diminish "queerness."

Bilbo is "very rich and very peculiar," largely because of his perpetual youth (1: 43), both of which make him seem different, queer: "It isn't natural, and trouble will come of it!" (1: 43). Part of this "trouble" results from social inequities that his wealth and good physical fortune exacerbate. In addition, however, Bilbo is "queer" to the other inhabitants of the Shire (1: 77) because he has been changed by his travels—his knowledge of the world—and by his possession of the Ring, which has stretched him thin (i.e., his awareness of moral issues—his knowledge of good and evil—has been expanded by having carried the Ring for so long). The tug between the desire of the self for the Ring (for the "Precious," or for what the self wishes to incorporate into the self) and the hobbit's desire to think of others beyond himself—to protect the Shire and the world by keeping the Ring hidden from Sauron's eye—has made him thin. It is no accident that the natural wearing of the Ring on the finger renders its wearer invisible, for when the Ring masters its wearer, it totally erases the *identity* of the wearer, and he becomes without a self. Unfortunately Bilbo never connected any change in the Ring with the Ring itself, instead taking "credit for that to himself, and he was very proud of it. Though he was getting restless and uneasy. *Thin and stretched* he said. A sign that the ring was getting control" (1: 77). Ironically the Ring appeals to the desires of the self for gold, power, love, as a means of mastering that individual.

The anticipated "trouble" is, however, averted in part by Baggins's generosity. He shares his money with his friends and relatives: "He had many devoted admirers among the hobbits of poor and unimportant families" (1: 43). Again, generously sharing his fortune allays the fears of difference among the less fortunate hobbits. He is considered "well-spoken," polite, and gentle, largely because, as well-off as he is, he treats his servant the Gaffer (Sam Gamgee's father) with great deference for his knowledge—reversing the usual master-servant relationship: "Bilbo was very polite to him, calling him 'Master Hamfast,' and consulting him constantly upon the growing of vegetables—in the matter of 'roots,' especially potatoes, the Gaffer was recognized as the leading authority by all in the neighbourhood (including himself)" (1: 44–45). Bilbo's sensitivity to the lower social class of his servant allows him to balance out their relationship through his genteel deference to the authority his servant does demonstrate, knowledge of vegetable growing. Bilbo has also taught the gardener's son Sam to read (1: 47)—a Middle-earth reflection of the Victorian ideal of educating the poor. The mutual respect of the hobbit aristocrat and the gardening servant-authority underscores Bilbo's gifts as an astute politician.

Two major social problems engage the political skills of Bilbo. First is the arrival of Frodo, an orphan and his heir, which causes the Sackville-Bagginses (Bilbo's other close heirs) consternation because their expected inheritance will presumably be reduced. Second is the necessary inheritance of Bag End (and its "treasure") by Frodo, predicated on the disappearance of Bilbo at the advanced age of 111 after a magnificent Birthday Party. Because of the continued enmity of the detested Sackville-Bagginses after the disappearance, Frodo will inherit these same familial problems requiring *his* political skills.

The Birthday Party, in the Shire, represents a symbolic paradigm for the ideal relationship between master and servant, wealthy aristocrat and members of the populace. As a site for potential self-aggrandizement and indulgence—which would not have been tolerated by the inhabitants within had they been either not invited or invited but expected to bring gifts—its signification for the political hobbit Bilbo is to mark the abundance of self-confidence, largess of the self, by *giving* gifts to all who attend and by offering them the splendor of fireworks, songs, dances, music, games, and fine and abundant food. It is, then, the perfect symbolic and political moment for Bilbo to disappear—that is, his largess signifies the disappearance of *selfishness* and masks his literal individual disappearance. At this party no one is not invited, and every guest is given presents, in the hobbit fashion (1: 50). Indeed, the liberality of Bilbo in inviting everyone to his Birthday Party is, as the Gaffer reminds the suspicious and manipulative Sandyman, another, more positive aspect of Bilbo's "queerness." The party thus also symbolizes Bilbo's enduring political concern for others—he is noble, a true gentleman, *because* he thinks only of others. And hobbits, who have the custom of giving presents to others on their own birthdays, are in general the least acquisitive of beings. The Sackville-Bagginses—Otho and his wife, Lobelia—attend even though they "disliked Bilbo and detested Frodo" (1: 57), largely because of the magnificence of the invitation.

Politic Bilbo in his speech to the hobbits expresses his fondness for them all and praises them as "excellent and admirable" (1: 54). This speech is important, for the occasion also honors his heir-nephew's birthday, which means Frodo will come of age and therefore Bilbo must make his disappearance. But even generous Bilbo, as a natural aristocrat, has difficulty in ridding himself entirely of the Ring—hobbit that he is, he is still related to the Sackville-Bagginses and thus shares in their (even for hobbits) excessive greed. Desire is a part of what the Ring represents.

The Ring of course works its power—illustrating the nature of the novel as a work about power—because more than anything it wishes to return to its maker-master and therefore wants to be put on (to make the wearer *naturally* invisible but supernaturally visible to the Eye of Sauron). In relation to the individual, then, possessing the Ring means that the individual loses sense of who he is and what he truly wants.

Bilbo initially has difficulty giving up the Ring—he wants to keep it, or the Ring wants him to—and he loses sight of that facility of the Ring, which makes him mistrust others as different and therefore (as with Sandyman) not with-me, for-me: "'Now it comes to it, I don't like parting with it at all, I may say. And I don't really see why I should. Why do you want me to?' he asked, and a curious change came over his voice. It was sharp with suspicion and annoyance. 'You are always badgering me about my ring: but you have never bothered me about the other things that I got on my journey" (1: 59). Bilbo wants to keep the Ring because it is his—he found it: "It is my own. I found it. It came to me" (1: 59). The specialness of the Ring—and therefore the specialness it confers on its owner—enhances the self, fills him with the illusion of power. And perhaps that specialness is what has made him "queer" to others. It is the last gift, the one he most has to give away—first to Gandalf and then to his heir Frodo. As with Frodo on Mount Doom, however, fighting first with himself and then with Gollum, Bilbo resists Gandalf as an adversary, using the same language as Gollum: "It is mine, I tell you. My own. My precious. Yes, my precious" (1: 59).

To free himself Bilbo has to let it go—which he finds difficult. Gandalf's demand for the Ring (as it lies on the mantel) arouses Bilbo's suspicions and fear that the wizard is a thief. Gandalf wins him over by saying, "I am not trying to rob you, but to help you. I wish you would trust me as you used" (1: 60). Bilbo apologizes: "But I felt so *queer*. . . . And I don't seem able to make up my mind" (1: 60–61).

What does the queerness represent, if not Bilbo's power in the Shire, which he regrets giving up—his power as "lord"? His specialness as an individual, the reason he is young perpetually, wealthy, generous? It is an enabler. For this reason it is difficult for Bilbo to give up the Ring, and yet death—which Bilbo's "disappearance" ultimately signifies—is what we all must pass through, to give up ourselves. Renunciation is the final gift—to allow the self to grow and mature, one must learn to be selfless. Thus the "presents" given to Bilbo's relatives are all "corrective" gifts, intended to change vices in the relatives (a pen and ink bottle to a relative who never answers letters, for example): "The poorer hobbits, and especially those of Bagshot Row, did very well" (1: 65).

The present Bilbo gives his nephew Frodo is similar in function—the Ring. With this possession comes the necessity for the quest—no "gift" at all but an unequalled opportunity for maturation. Frodo at age 50 (when Gandalf pronounces the need for the quest to return the Ring) "comes of age," becomes himself, an individual, but in this narrative, unlike the normal bildungsroman on which this work is modeled, he must *return* his "gift" to its maker, Mount Doom—such a return, the ultimate hobbit birthday gift—to its "mother" source rather than its "father" owner Sauron. Instead of going on a quest to obtain some knowledge or thing, he goes to divest himself (and the world) of this power. In life maturity means the loss of the child into adulthood. This quest reverses that idea: the adult Frodo (age 50) must attempt to recuperate the child, as the Ring returns to its origin.

What does this quest signify? We have established that the political hobbit we see in Bilbo "rules" his Shire through self-abnegation and generosity; however, the rule implied by the Ring is entirely different. As the inscription testifies, it allows for differences—elves, dwarves, men—but only because there is One Ring intended to align their differences:

> One Ring to rule them all, One Ring to find them,
> One Ring to bring them all and in the darkness bind them,
> In the Land of Mordor where the Shadows lie.
>
> (1: 81)

Returning the Ring to its origin means refusal of power as domination of the One—of sameness—and acceptance of power as respect for difference and diversity. It is Frodo, more different even than his unnatural uncle Bilbo, who is better suited to this quest.

Different from Bilbo because of his mother's dark familial roots in the Old Forest, Frodo may be acceptable to the Shire only because of his uncle Bilbo's wealth and favor. Like his uncle Bilbo Baggins, Frodo is "queer." Most interestingly of all, Frodo Baggins begins his fictive life (as his creator does his maturity) an orphan and (also like his creator) an orphan from "across the river." He is a Baggins from Hobbiton, but his mother was a Brandybuck from Buckland, "where folks are so queer," says Old Noakes (1: 45). Their "queerness" is caused by living on the wrong side of the Brandywine River, next to the Old Forest, and also by the fact that they use boats on the big river, which "isn't natural," says the Gaffer, at least for hobbits (1: 45).

Indeed, Frodo's father, Drogo Baggins, was a "decent respectable hobbit" until he drowned in an uncustomary river outing. Drogo and Miss Primula Brandybuck (Bilbo's first cousin on his mother's side) took out a boat one night after a grand dinner at the home of his father-in-law, Old Gorbadoc, and either Drogo's weight sank the boat or Primula pushed him in (1: 46).

After Bilbo's disappearance—that is, his successful self-renunciation—Frodo's first test as Lord of the Manor comes of course from the Sackville-Bagginses (who offer him low prices for other things not given away and who spread rumors that Gandalf and Frodo conspired to get Bilbo's wealth). That Frodo can tolerate difference is symbolically clear to the reader (if not to Lobelia Sackville-Baggins) because he is accompanied by his cousin Merry Brandybuck—like his mother, from Buckville near the Old Forest. But Frodo mistakenly assumes at first that Bag End is his "inheritance"—his for keeping.

As time passes Frodo perpetuates Bilbo's reputation for "oddity" (1: 70) by continuing to give Birthday Parties for his uncle. His closest friends are Merry Brandybuck (from the queer Brandy-bucks), Peregrin Took, and other younger hobbits who had descended from the Old Took and had been fond of Bilbo (1: 71). (Bilbo's mother was a Took.) Like Bilbo, Frodo preserves his youth, so much so that when he is 50 the Shire inhabitants begin to think him "queer."

This tension between the "normal" and the "queer" hobbit will blossom into the ethical drama of *Rings* in later chapters and books. The question Tolken addresses is this: How can individuals (and nations) so different from one another coexist in harmony? The danger is clear: the Brandybucks will be forever stigmatized by the Shire inhabitants because they choose to live beyond the river in unhobbitlike fashion. And what is to prevent a Dark Hobbit Lord from then using this Shire fear of difference to separate the Brandybucks from the Bagginses? to divide one family branch from another, to insist that all must be the same and live within the Shire? to act and to think and to dress as all the Shire inhabitants?

Difference, for Tolkien, leads to recklessness (the unusual youthful Frodo stealing mushrooms and venturing into others' lands), adventure (Bilbo and Frodo going off on their respective journeys), and ultimately wisdom and understanding. Difference can also be social—the difference between a Baggins and a Gamgee, which is artificial and serves no valid purpose if used to separate the two. The validity of lower-class occupations (e.g., gardening, domestic service) is ultimately certified by Sam's heroism, as he carries Frodo up Mount Doom, just as Gollum's moral deficiency is validated by his final contribution to civilization and cosmic good when he disobeys his Master and steals the Ring. The servant—Sam or Gollum—ultimately contributes as much or more to Middle-earth than the Master Frodo. For Tolkien it is the generosity of the Master but also his obverse chief weaknesses—pride and avarice—that depend on and demand the unflagging support and dedicated valor of the humble servant, whose chief strength is his humility and whose chief weakness is his lack of self-assertion. Tolkien's point is that each serves the other; where the difference of one ends, the complementary difference of the other begins. The relationship is circular and yet based on both need and desire, necessity and obligation, the dance of Self and Other, until the music ends.

Despite his initially seeming different, Gollum is in a sense a type of distant hobbit, an alter ego for Bilbo-Frodo (just as the Cain-and-Abel parable of Deagol-Smeagol emphasizes family murder and cousin hate). And so Gollum, like Frodo, regards the Ring as his Birthday Present because he acquires it on that special day. For Frodo Gollum is the Shire equivalent of a Brandybuck, and the hobbit reacts to the idea of Gollum as Sandyman did to him—by suspecting Gollum's strangeness, his "queerness." Frodo wishes Gollum had been killed long ago (1: 92), not understanding the mercy or pity that stayed Bilbo's hand and therefore (ironically) the same mercy or pity that will save *him* on the lip of Mount Doom. Even more ironically it is Gollum's disobedience toward his "Master" Frodo at Mount Doom—only in a greater and providential sense to be construed as mercy or pity—that saves Frodo. And it is not that Gollum's (or Frodo's) hand is stayed—ironically it is his finger that is bitten off, with the Ring still attached, that saves Frodo and also Middle-earth.

If we look more closely at the role of minor characters, the tension of difference between Self and Other, familiar and unlike, becomes more clear-cut. Tolkien's joy in creating characters is to reverse suspicious expectation in his "heroes" and in his readers. For example, it is not clear to Frodo whether Farmer *Maggot* is friend or foe (1: 132): his name suggests a disgusting creature associated with the eggs of flies and decaying organic matter, death, the earth. And to adult Frodo, whose youthful memories recall the anger of Maggot and his dogs over the theft of mushrooms, Farmer Maggot looms as an adversary. Maggot, however, provides a different point of view for Frodo when he recalls Frodo as "reckless," one of the "worst young rascals" (1: 136). The truth is that a protective Maggot has shielded the hobbits from the inquiries of a hooded Black Rider and also that the recklessness of youthful Frodo foreshadows his present heroics and venture into Mordor. Nevertheless, Farmer Maggot remains a hobbit whose advice to Frodo now reflects the typical suspiciousness of the Shire: "You should never have gone mixing yourself up with Hobbiton Folk, Mr. Frodo. Folk are *queer* up there" (1: 136; my italics).

Furthermore, Frodo's fellow hobbits Merry and Pippin and his servant Sam have "conspired" (Tolkien's word) behind Frodo's back to accompany him on his journey. This normally pejorative "conspiracy" occurs despite Frodo's protective attempts to keep the purpose of his mission (and the existence of the Ring) a secret from them. His misguided attempts to shield them from danger seriously underestimate their own "queerness" (for Brandybucks and Tooks live beyond the river next to the Old Forest) and thus their own potential for heroism and adventure (to say nothing of their common hobbit desire to serve, epitomized in the gardener Sam Gamgee, the most modest, socially and personally, of them all). In *The Lord of the Rings* difference, fueled by the power of words, polarizes the forces of good and evil, social class, and political group.

6

The Political Hobbit:
The Fellowship of the Ring

LANGUAGE MADE POLITICAL

The word *queer* serves powerfully to fix and type Bilbo and then Frodo for some of the inhabitants of Hobbiton, illustrating the ability of language to exert control over others by playing on their fears of difference and that which is foreign. Tolkien well understood the power of the written and spoken word, philologist that he was— he knew that words were magic. As his former student S. T. R. O. d'Ardenne has noted, "Tolkien belonged to that very rare class of linguists, now becoming extinct, who . . . could understand and recapture the glamour of 'the Word.' 'In the beginning was the Word, and the Word was with God, and the Word was God.'"[47] For Tolkien words provide the means to unify and extend the social community, to understand the various species of nature, and to cross the boundaries of time (past and present) and space (the equivalent of earthly, supernal, and infernal in Middle-earth).

As early as *Fellowship* language becomes a bond between potentially or literally diverse groups: the Inn of Bree is a meeting place for the "idle, talkative, and inquisitive" (1: 207). And those able to understand more than one language or to communicate in one language eloquently frequently surpass their peers in the heroic nature of their accomplishments. The Rangers, for example, not only cross geographic boundaries but also understand the languages of beasts and birds, a facility that enables them in their

37

occupation; it is no accident that from them Aragorn the King comes. And Frodo is actually moved to sing a nursery-rhyme-like song—about the Man in the Moon and a merry old inn—at the Sign of the Prancing Pony in Bree. Pretending to be interested in history and geography in order to mask his real purpose of returning the Ring to Mordor (1: 213), Frodo uses language—words, that is—in a composition that has underlying personal meaning. The Man in the Moon gets drunk, and the ostler observes that he's "drowned his wits" (1: 217), nearly leading to disaster, much like the excessive drinking of Frodo's own father that did indeed lead to his drowning.

Not surprisingly Frodo's moral and political education throughout the novel, but especially in the first volume, is reflected in his heightened perception of the trickiness of appearances and language. Interestingly, Sam the Gardener seems to possess this sensitivity from the beginning: Sam does not like Bill Ferny, a true rogue, from first sight (1: 224), whereas Frodo, initially at least, naively and incorrectly imagines that Strider (actually Aragorn) is a rogue wanting money. Against truly destructive and evil powers, Frodo as the learned Mr. Underhill and Sam as his equally literate valet (taught his letters by Bilbo) pretend to a heroism into which they are educated only gradually.

For Tolkien the hobbits' moral and political development is reflected in their own growing artistry, from the silliness of naive rhymes to the complexity of later songs that echo those in ancient and medieval epics. Indeed, many of the initial songs in *Rings* are drawn from the epics about Middle-earth, composed or translated by Bilbo the Master Singer, memorized by the faithful Sam, and used to inspire and educate those in the present. It is Sam who sings of Gil-galad the Elven-King whose star fell into the darkness of Mordor, when the Fellowship comes on the "tumbled ring" of Weathertop, formerly the watchtower called Amon Sûl (1: 251). Bilbo in fact translated this song from the epic *The Fall of Gil-galad* in the "ancient tongue" (1: 251) and taught it to Sam.

We shall first look at the use of language and song as a means of moral and political education for the hobbits and concomitantly the physical and moral threat to them posed through language by various adversaries in book 1. We shall then examine the same pattern when it occurs in book 2, after the hobbits have been joined by other species to form the Fellowship at the Council of Elrond.

LANGUAGE AND INDIVIDUALITY IN BOOK 1

In the first book language is a restorative, recuperating the energy of the past. The words of Tom Bombadil, described as an "ancient language" of "wonder and delight" (1: 202), provide a model for Frodo and Sam: they embody the power to communicate with plants, animals, and all species; they function magically to work good at times of danger and crisis (that is, when Frodo and the hobbits are trapped by Old Man Willow and again by the barrow-wights); and they mirror the innate joy and harmony in the creation of the world known as Middle-earth. Tom Bombadil and his mate Goldberry early on in the book reveal a verbal means of restoring natural order and harmony through reminders of a species's natural obligations and role: "Eat earth! Dig deep! Drink water!" (1: 169), directed to Old Man Willow as he attempts to transcend his place in the created order, for the Old Forest represents the survivors of Woods "when Trees were lords" (1: 181), and therefore their pride—wisdom—and malice assert themselves. As Eldest, Tom Bombadil—older even than the Old Forest—acts as an Adam the Namer who knows the history of the created world and remembers the orginal ideal for each species. In more iconic form he therefore resembles his hobbit friend Farmer Maggot, who also has earth (and clay) under his feet, earth-tiller that he is (1: 184). Even Goldberry's wish for the hobbits' safe journey (1: 188) is charmlike: "Speed now, fair guests! . . And hold to your purpose! North with the wind in the left eye and a blessing on your footsteps! Make haste while the Sun shines!" (1: 188). Full of the power and knowledge of Nature, Tom and Goldberry themselves, as the master and mistress of wood, water, and hill, wear garments in colors reflective of the elements and regions. He wears a blue jacket with yellow boots (1: 173), and Goldberry, daughter of the River, wears a silver-green dress and shoes of fish-mail (1: 174).

Frodo, as if he has learned how to sing appropriately and naturally from Tom's models, celebrates the signification of Goldberry (and her implicit bond with Tom) in a joyous paean:

O slender as a willow-wand! O clearer than clear water!
O reed by the living pool! Fair river-daughter!
O spring-time and summer-time, and spring again after!
O wind on the waterfall, and the leaves' laughter!

(1: 173)

Again influenced by Tom's harmonies, Frodo begins dreaming about this same time (1: 177). His vision has turned inward, to the subconscious, and his perception of Gandalf's peril through dream marks the power to visualize, articulated only during the natural function of sleep as a restorative power.

Ironically it is *sleep* that blots out consciousness when the questers enter the Old Forest and when they encounter the barrow-wights: sleep that is closer to death and unnatural in the middle of the day. In the Old Forest the sleep of instinctive life is impelled by Old Man Willow, rooted in one place, to those he envies for their ability to move, travel, and speak. If man (as Aristotle said and medieval civilization believed) is a rational animal, then speech is what separates human beings from animals and plants. There is also a "language" spoken here, although it is indigenous to a much more rooted life form. Note too that only Sam the Gardener is not hurt by Old Man Willow, perhaps because he respects Sam's knowledge of roots and vegetable growth: Sam is to Old Man Willow nearly as Bilbo was to Sam's father, the Gaffer.

The second threat—the fog on the barrow-downs (chapter 8)—clouds vision and conceals the barrow-wights. The cold voice from the ground that threatens Frodo intones, "I am waiting for you" (1: 193)—enough to freeze his bones and make him lose consciousness, a "spell" that reveals a kind of dark wordless and death-dealing artistry. It is as if the underside of Nature has been given a voice: "Suddenly a song began: a cold murmur, rising and falling. The voice seemed far away and immeasurably dreary. . . . Out of the formless stream of sad but horrible sounds, strings of words would now and again shape themselves: grim, hard, cold words, heartless and miserable. The night was *railing* against the morning of which it was bereaved, and the cold was *cursing* the warmth for which it hungered" (1: 194–95; my italics). The actual spell invokes the powers of death and diminution: the incantation of the wights ("cold be hand and heart and bone / and cold be sleep under stone" [1: 195]) reminds us of the power of death and devastation—the withering of land and nation—equivalent in the moral sphere to the power of the Dark Lord. To use language to hurt others is the mark of the powerless—if one is an insignificant Sandyman—but to curse others with the coldness of hand and heart is to harm the living, life itself, and is the mark of that which hates life:

> Cold be hand and heart and bone,
> and cold be sleep under stone:
> never more to wake on stony bed,
> never, till the Sun fails and the Moon is dead.
> In the black wind the stars shall die,
> and still on gold here let them lie,
> till the dark lord lifts his hand
> over dead sea and withered land.
>
> (1: 195)

The spell is Tolkien's means of revealing the animism of nature, but it serves the Neoplatonic purpose of defining Nature as a book—veiling the immanent Word of God. That the Great Barrows provide burial mounds for the kings and queens of old means that the barrow-wights are probably lost, dead (Anglo-Saxon?) kings whose envy of the living is impotent—hence the words they use to instill fear in the hobbits, words inviting paralysis and impotence. (And indeed Frodo feels turned to stone [1: 195]). After he rescues them this second time, Tom describes the barrow-wights as "sons of forgotten kings walking in loneliness, guarding from evil things folk that are heedless" (1: 201), specifically the men of Westernesse overcome by the evil king of Carn Dûm. In Tom's vision the hobbits see men on a "vast shadowy plain" and carrying bright swords, one of the men bearing a star on his brow (1: 201).

As budding artists whose knowledge of good and evil is necessary to create, the hobbit company is just beginning to learn to envision figuratively. The artistry of the small fellowship reflects Tom's tutelage. To repel the fog on the barrow-downs the hobbit company sings a song as a means of rescue/salvation—"Then he [Bombadil] taught them a rhyme to sing, if they should by ill-luck fall into any danger or difficulty the next day":

Ho! Tom Bombadil, Tom Bombadillo!
By water, wood and hill, by reed and willow,
By fire, sun and moon, harken now and hear us!
Come, Tom Bombadil, for our need is near us!

(1: 186)

And Frodo, when the hobbits are among the barrow-wights, tries to rescue his followers. After he cuts his hand, he calls for Tom Bombadil (1: 196), whose own "rescue" consists *only* of songs banishing darkness and cold and celebrating light, truth, and good (1: 197):

Get out, you old Wight! Vanish in the sunlight!
Shrivel like the cold mist, like the winds go wailing,
Out into the barren lands far beyond the mountains!
Come never here again! Leave your barrow empty!
Lost and forgotten be, darker than the darkness,
Where gates stand for ever shut, till the world is mended.

(1: 197)

And:

Wake now my merry lads! Wake and hear me calling!
Warm now be heart and limb! The cold stone is fallen;
Dark door is standing wide; dead hand is broken.
Night under Night is flown, and the Gate is open!

(1: 197)

The earliest form of heroic poetry was probably incantation and charm; Tom Bombadil's lively charm rejuvenates the hobbits from the sleep of loss and forgetfulness—they awaken.

Throughout this drama of the symbolic value of language, letters from the principals convey important clues, messages, instructions; species subverted and transformed by evil—the Black Riders, for example—lose their ability to speak along with their ability to choose good and evil and their ability to act independently. These Riders (fallen men) hiss and mutter rather than talk (1: 235). Their strength exists in darkness and loneliness (1: 236), as if they symbolized despair, ultimate irrationality, which for most of us means nothingness, inhumanity, or what is described as the abyss, a kind of chaos. And the clues the company follows in tracing Gandalf's path are written in a kind of language—scratches in runes that reveal his time there—and their presence is ambiguous. Did Gandalf falter? Is the clue intentional? Being unable to decipher past clues—written recently in scratches and dots among the stones in the past, or written above the Gate to Moria in an alien tongue long ago—is part of the dilemma of the scholar-hero, who lapses into occasional bouts of despair, loneliness, and homesickness, as when the Fellowship is uncertain whether Gandalf was present at Weathertop and if he was in danger (1: 253). Tolkien associates their isolation and fear with lack of communication, contrasting it with the laughter of past togetherness at home and at the Inn of Bree.

Finally, the knowledge conferred on the wearer of the Ring carries with it power—that is, knowledge *is* power. For example, after the Fellowship builds a fire in the dark in the dell near the Road (chapter 11, "A Knife in the Dark"), Strider recites the tale of Tinúviel and explains the history of mortal Beren and his immortal beloved Lúthien Tinúviel: the power of song overcomes the fear of the dark and dark powers. But when Sam senses danger, meaning the presence of the Dark Riders, dread overwhelms Frodo, and terror flattens Merry and Pippin. Frodo is then mastered by the desire to put on the Ring—to conquer ignorance, to *see*, to know: "Immediately, though everything else remained as before, dim and dark, the shapes became terribly clear" (1: 263). The Ring with its power to cross dimensions, as it were, carries with it the double danger of two worlds. When the other world becomes immanent within this one, it is through the ability to cross one mode into another, or the power of the Ring, that Frodo becomes apparent in that world, though invisible in the normal world.

As symbol of the power of language (sounds or written signs organized into a pattern that emanate from one person and pass to another and convey meaning), the Ring also suggests the danger of such power—that one will be understood, "seen," apparent, and therefore vulnerable to attack. The Ring (language, representing the means to knowledge) counters terror and despair (irrationality) but can lead to physical danger and spiritual debilitation while the inner self eventually strengthens. Its possession implies the Faustian bargain—becoming godlike, granted magical powers of knowledge, in exchange for the loss of one's soul. That the wound of the

Enemy transcends the merely physical is suggested by the poisonous wound of Frodo in chapter 11 physically healed by Aragorn with *athelas*, but because of its transcendent evil making him shiver and dream of "endless dark wings" (1: 273). As the Fellowship members continue their journey into the destroyed and ruined land, they return to the Past to their dreamed heritage (note that they came on the stone trolls about whom Bilbo had so often told them).

The climax of book 1 crowns its last chapter, "The Flight to the Ford," when the ultimate threat is to be struck dumb, paralyzed, to lack all language and therefore all action—to be made stone. To counter this threat, the opposite needs to happen—enlivened and inspired, the flesh will become word. That is exactly what happens when Frodo confronts the Dark Riders at the bottom of the hill ("Underhill") and fears crossing the Ford to Rivendell without being ambushed by others. Frodo demands that they return to Mordor (1: 285) when they call to him to "Come back!," promising to take him to Mordor; they cry, "The Ring!" with "deadly voices," but Frodo counters with an oath "By Elbereth and Lúthien the Fair" and lifts his sword (1: 286). It is at this point that "Frodo was stricken dumb. He felt his tongue cleave to his mouth, and his heart labouring" (1: 286). He is saved, of course, by Gandalf the wizard, whose possession of one of the Elven Rings is sufficient to fill the black horses with madness. Again, the danger is the stilling of language, the death of the Word. The flesh is made word by means of supernatural agency—epitomized in that "shining figure of white light," Gandalf (1: 286). To lose one's tongue is thus to lose one's rationality, selfhood, self—and so the Dark Riders are also called "Ringwraiths," ghosts of their former glory.

In the second book it is, accordingly, speech, debate, and the exchange of words that signals the community that unites the Free Peoples and creates the Fellowship, beginning with the meeting at Elrond's. The second book, then, acts as complement to and mirror image of the first. It marks the completion of Frodo's transformation, into the political hobbit he must become to survive.

LANGUAGE AND DEMOCRACY IN BOOK 2

At Rivendell Frodo learns how the Ring changes perception, particularly of the Other, makes that Other seem "queer," different, and antagonistic to the self. When Bilbo asks Frodo to see the Ring, Frodo is reluctant to show it to his uncle: "To his distress and amazement he found that he was no longer looking at Bilbo; a shadow seemed to have fallen between them, and through it he found himself eyeing a little wrinkled creature with a hungry face and bony groping hands. He felt a desire to strike him" (1: 306). Tolkien imaginatively reconstructs the psychology of selfishness, self-centeredness, and cupidity. Of course the "shadow" is literally provided by the controlling Ring, but as shadow it is linked to the inarticulate and dark Ringwraiths and the paralyzed humanity they signify. The Ring's power here cripples one's higher nature and alters perception of the Other in a way that prohibits union and camaraderie.

To a political person the Ring's power effectively stifles democracy. Thus bearing it, as Frodo does, provides the greatest challenge to his political education. If he turns away from the Other, is the repudiation his own free choice and not shadowed by the power of the Ring? How can Frodo learn to distinguish true vision and perception from false? Book 2 gives the reader a model for democracy at the Council at Elrond's house and a model for the true vision of the leader at Lothlórien. But it is only at the end, when Boromir, a seemingly loyal member of the Fellowship, tests Frodo that Tolkien indicates the extent of the hobbit's progress.

The meeting with the folk at Rivendell opens with songs rather than political speeches, reflective of the elves' appetite for music and tales and of their link with Tom Bombadil and Goldberry as positive models: "At first the beauty of the melodies and the interwoven words in the Elven-tongue, even though he understood them little, held him in a spell, as soon as he began to attend to them. Almost it seemed that the words took shape, and visions of far lands and bright things that he had never yet imagined opened out before him, and the firelit hall became like a golden mist above seas of foam that sighed upon the margins of the world" (1: 307). The sleep into which he sinks resembles that of the Old Forest and the barrow-wights, catalyzed as they are by animistic and instinctive forces (Old Man Willow), the dark underside of the same natural energy (the wights), or the supernatural and magical power of the elves. Here Frodo will learn about the past of all species and all creation, just as he has learned in book 1 about the private past of Bilbo and the hobbit-linked history of the Ring (that is, beginning with Gollum) in the Shire at the time of the Birthday Party. He will learn, however, from the magic words of the elves and of the tale-teller Bilbo rather than those of the wizard Gandalf alone, as he did in the first book.

The actual Council is somber: many peoples have heard of the Ring and of the movements of the Enemy, but, given this past history, how can the Free World counter Sauron? Initially the peoples (or at least this messenger) must debate a solution, despite Boromir's suspicions that Frodo's ring is not *the* Ring, and the ignorance or incomplete information of many of the other peoples. The success of the Council occurs in part because of the modesty (or at least rhetorical pose of modesty) of Gandalf and Aragorn. Gandalf confesses he was at fault for letting the words of Saruman lull him (1: 329); Aragorn recounts how he aided Gandalf in the search for Gollum, "since it seemed fit that Isildur's heir should labour to repair Isildur's fault" (1: 330). The public admission of guilt enhances the speakers' credibility and weakens any suspicions that the two may have been seeking their own gain.

Furthermore, when such old enmities as the one between the elves and dwarves erupt into conflict, Gandalf the leader wisely attempts to keep the meeting on track and to the matter at hand—the recounting of the discovery of the Ring. Most important, however, he asks openly for solutions to the problem of how to fight the rising power—whether to give the Ring to Bombadil, "oldest and fatherless" (1: 347), to keep it in one of the elven regions (Imladris, the Havens, or Lórien), to destroy it, to send it over the Sea, to hide the Ring, or to "unmake it" (1: 350). After much debate Elrond does hit upon a solution—to take "a hard road, a road unforeseen. There lies our hope, if hope it be. To walk into peril—to Mordor. We must send the Ring to the Fire" (1: 350). Only with the helpful exchanges of the many does the group work logically through all the possibilities to the one solution Sauron will never imagine, so unlike his desire is it ("But the only measure that he knows is desire, desire for power; and so he judges all hearts" [1: 353]). Once the Council fully realizes that the "very desire of it corrupts the heart" (1: 350), it may also select the most appropriate Ringbearer, from the smallest and least greedy species—the hobbits.

One of the last to speak, Frodo volunteers to bear the Ring with a sense of misgiving and a "longing to rest and remain at peace by Bilbo's side" (1: 353). He has volunteered because Elrond has argued that "small hands" may "move the wheels of the world" if the "eyes of the great" look elsewhere (1: 353). And Sam, hidden in a corner out of sight, also volunteers, out of concern for his master rather than for the Free World (1: 355). They are not forced to volunteer, but they do so of their own volition, knowing that there is no one else. Democracy in this Council means that the humblest (at least seemingly so) may be chosen for the most heroic of journeys.

Joined by other representatives of the Free Peoples, Frodo and Sam eventually arrive at the Mines of Moria, whose opening is hidden by an invisible door with a secret password. Words, speeches, songs—all serve an important role in *Rings*, especially as a weapon counter to the wordlessness, the power, sought by Sauron and Saruman. (It is no accident that the three elven rings, unlike the One Ring, "were not made as weapons of war or conquest: that is not their power. Those who made them did not desire strength or domination or hoarded wealth, but understanding, making, and healing, to preserve all things unstained" [1: 352]). The power of words throughout this book aids that preservation and understanding. At the door to the Mines, speaking the word *friend* allows the company ingress and hence the continued progress of the Ringbearer. Gandalf describes this key as "absurdly simple, like most riddles when you see the answer" (1: 401).

The dwarf mines have been the scene of battle and attack as a result of Durin's Bane, the desire for *mithril* symbolized by the crown of stars that appeared above his head when he peered into the pool of Mirrormere (1: 411). That is, in the city of Dwarrowdelf the precious jewels and metals Durin's folk delved—especially *mithril*—were "the foundation of their wealth, so also it was their destruction: they delved too greedily and too deep, and disturbed that from which they fled, Durin's Bane" (1: 413). The "sleep" in which Durin passed (1: 412) is marked now by a crown of sunken stars in Mirrormere—his crown lies in the water. The sleep that resulted from Durin's desire resembles the dark sleep characteristic of the Old Forest, or the sleep of the barrow-wights, but the physical death for which it acts as image also has a psychological correlative and is linked with the shadow, darkness, and ghostliness of the Ringwraiths. One other "riddle" that the dwarves have often puzzled over is here deciphered when they read Daeron's Runes on Balin's tomb—and thus realize that Balin, descendant of Durin, also succumbed to the Bane. The recovery of the lost past in a way offers the clear light of realization and understanding in exchange for the darkness of ignorance and the unknown. And the company's exploration of the Mines is a trek into the past as recorded on doors, tombs, and even books, including a history of Balin's folk (1: 417ff.), the Book of Mazarbul.

Throughout this episode the monstrous desire that drove Durin and then Balin is often identified with a monster correlative. For example, Gandalf says, when they are pursued by mysterious drumbeats, "I am afraid Balin is buried deep, and maybe something else is buried there too" (1: 425). This monstrosity may also be identified with the Balrog who attacks the company and who is battled to the death by Gandalf. Tolkien's lack of specific definition and description for this monster enhances his power to intimidate: "Something was coming up behind them. What it was could not be seen: it was like *a great shadow*, in the middle of which was a dark form, *of man-shape maybe*, yet greater; and a power and terror seemed to be in it and to go before it" (1: 428; my italics). Identified only as having a "streaming mane" and holding a blade and a whip, the Balrog symbolizes inarticulate violence fired by atavistic, primordial wrath. It *is* the Shadow, everyone's alter ego, that dark self which figures primarily in the hobbit species through Gollum. Left behind after the destruction of civilization and decorum, the Balrog represents the chief threat to community, to fellowship—that violence which destroys and disorders. Incarnate Otherness in his human shapelessness, Balrog sums up difference within this company and foreshadows physically the threat to its mission that will be provided by Boromir at the end of book 1. Or, as Haldir the elf says when he blindfolds Legolas at Lórien, "in nothing is the power of the Dark Lord more clearly shown than in the estrangement that divides all those who still oppose him" (1: 451).

The antidote for this pursuit of the company by hellish orcs, trolls, and the Balrog is the peaceful and healing sojourn with the elves in Lothlórien (chapter 6). The blindness of Durin recalled at Moria in Mirrormere is exchanged for the clear prospects of the visionary mirror belonging to Galadriel, Lady of Lothlórien and holder of one of the elven rings. If the Balrog signals monstrous community dysfunction, then Galadriel in contrast signals the principle of supernatural (even divine) communal wholeness and harmony. In exchange for the crown of Durin the company finds the crown of true peace and wisdom. Paradisal in its seasonal changelessness, with golden leaves in its Golden Wood and an otherworldly quality to its people, Lórien offers the company a haven from the marauding dangers of the cruel outside world as well as a threat to evil (1: 439).

Although the world changed even for Lórien when the "Dwarves awakened evil in the mountains" (1: 442), the elves who inhabit it still dwell in the trees (*Mellyrn*) but rarely now encounter other folk (1: 444) and thus seldom speak in any other tongue than their own. Their mistrust is not natural or typical of the elves, merely necessary. Nevertheless, "In Rivendell there was memory of ancient things, in Lórien the ancient things still lived on in the waking world" (1: 453). A world beyond time, Lórien also suggests "a world that was no more" (1: 453). Frodo imagines he has "stepped through a high window that looked on a vanished world" (1: 454), that he sees a world of clear-cut shapes in "fresh and poignant" colors "as if he had at that moment first perceived them and made for them names new and wonderful. In winter here no heart could mourn for summer or for spring. No blemish or sickness or deformity could be seen in anything that grew up on the earth" (1: 454–55). So perfect is this vision that he describes the experience as being "*inside* a song" (1: 455). Joy and happiness incarnate, Lórien offers the delight of living things, especially trees, and acceptance and toleration of all creation.

The restoring harmony of Lórien is reflected in the healing words of Lady Galadriel in greeting the ancient enemy of the elves, the dwarf Gimli. Because she uses the ancient dwarf names and mourns the loss of that past civilization, she endears herself to him: "fair were the many-pillared halls of the Khazad-dûm in Elder Days before the fall of mighty kings beneath the stone" (1: 461). In addition, when Gimli looks into her eyes, "it seemed to him that he looked into the heart of an enemy and saw there love and under-standing" (1: 461). Her sympathy for the dwarves and loving desire to accept all different from herself, even a traditional enemy, helps to heal old wounds, even those caused by Durin's Bane. That her own land has suffered as a result of his ancestor's fault makes even more remarkable her gentle words of welcome. Forgiveness, hospi-tality, understanding—all are qualities characteristic of Lady Galadriel that inspire Gimli's courteous praise of her and serve as a model of toleration for difference.

Galadriel's gentleness masks a stern wisdom that educates the individual members of the quest into the dangers they face: "For not in doing or contriving, nor in choosing between this course and another, can I avail; but only in knowing what was and is, and in part also what shall be" (1: 462). Her gaze at each of them ascer-tains their inner drives, the stuff of which they are made: Sam confesses, "I felt as if I hadn't got nothing on, and I didn't like it. She seemed to be looking inside me and asking me what I would do if she gave me the chance of flying back home to the Shire to a nice little hole" (1: 463). Through her gaze she tests Sam, Merry, Gimli, all the company. Ominously, only Boromir doubts her purposes, forgetting what Aragorn reminds them, that "there is in her and in this land no evil, unless a man bring it hither himself" (1: 464).

The wisdom she and her mirror represent already stretches Frodo's incipient artistry as songster, when "his thought took shape in a song that seemed fair to him," and Sam's childlike rhyme about rockets and fireworks (1: 465). For these two, whose hearts the Lady has rightly read as most courageous, the Mirror of Gal-adriel allows them real vision of what they desire and do not desire, to see, whether past, present, or future. Sam's vision presents the future pictures of Frodo asleep, Sandyman cutting trees, a factory in the Shire—threats to persons and places he loves and wishes to serve, all of which he *will* face in the future. Frodo's vision is appropriately grander but analogous to Sam's. He sees Gandalf alone and wandering, Bilbo restless, the Sea and a ship, the Eye of Sauron watching for him—gaze nearly meeting gaze (1: 471). Espe-cially the latter will test and nearly break him. To him as Ringbearer Galadriel reveals her elven ring, and to her Frodo the Ringbearer presents, inadvertently, his own test of her wisdom and judgment—he offers her the One Ring, although she rightly refuses, and thereafter she prophesies her own diminution and exile (1: 474).

Lórien, then, and the visionary Mirror of Galadriel both restore and test the company and the Ringbearer. Paradise may be a responsibility as well as a gift, a moral weight not evident in the calm house of Tom Bombadil and Goldberry in book 1 (the equivalent structural parallel in book 1). From Lórien the company members take gifts that will remind them of this regenerative halfway house—*lembas,* or waybread, that strengthens the body; elvish robes that are light and weather-sensitive to shield the wearers from an unfriendly gaze; and individual gifts that also remind the reader of the extravagant gift-giving at Bilbo's Birthday Party. Especially significant for the quest is the earth from Galadriel's orchard given to the gardener Sam and the phial of light from Eärendil's star given to Frodo that will lighten dark places (1: 488). The starlight and the earth will offer moral support, hope, and understanding redolent of the eternal springtime represented in Lórien. They constitute weapons that will aid the heroes in fighting against adversaries (e.g., Shelob) and in rebuilding Middle-earth (particularly the forests of the Shire). At the moment the most painful and moving gift is the strand of Galadriel's hair requested by the courteous dwarf Gimli. It symbolizes generosity, the antithesis to the avarice common to dwarves known as Durin's Bane. Galadriel acknowledges that "your hands shall flow with gold, and yet over you gold shall have no dominion" (1: 487). Gimli's transformation rests on a painful education about the real, internal peril of this quest: "I would not have come, had I known the danger of light and joy" (1: 490). To leave behind paradise is more difficult than never knowing it exists, because of the preciousness of its restorative power. The consolation Gimli (and the others) bear away is that of memory, as well as the acknowledgment of the inner nobility gained by voluntary renunciation.

Such strength of character, such courtesy, is not witnessed in the man Boromir, who fails to control his own desire for the Precious—the Ring. Because of his verbal assault and attack on Frodo near the top of the Hill of Sight, Amon Hen (chapter 10), the Fellowship is broken, the quests divided, Frodo and Sam fleeing in one direction and the remainder of the company in disarray. Boromir, the antitype of Gimli, deteriorates morally after the sojourn in

Lórien. His mistake is to privilege his own need for the Ring, ostensibly to protect Minas Tirith from the Enemy but in reality to express his racial hostility toward hobbits and his own sense of personal and national superiority. In his anger and pride he chastises Frodo and his mission to return the Ring to Mordor: "Obstinate fool! Running wilfully to death and ruining our cause. If any mortals have claim to the Ring, it is the men of Númenor, and not Halflings. It is not yours save by unhappy chance. It might have been mine. It should be mine. Give it to me!" (1: 516). The madness that seizes him distorts his perception so that he imagines hobbit Frodo as Other, different, a "miserable trickster" (1: 517) who will sell them all to Sauron.

Isolated as Frodo was at the Ford at the end of book 1 when he heroically resisted the Black Riders, Frodo at the end of book 2 reaches the summit of Amon Hen, climbs upon the ancient kings' throne like a "lost child," and, Ring on his finger, is granted misty visions like those seen in the Mirror of Galadriel—except that these visions are spatiotemporally organized by the geographic context of the Hill of the Eye of the Men of Númenor. Just as he was challenged by the Black Riders in book 1, here Frodo is challenged by the gaze of the Eye of Sauron. Resisting the power of that gaze—the power of hegemonic authority—he instead listens to a voice within and *chooses* to take off the Ring. The resistance strengthens his resolve to depart alone, which will ensure the success of his mission and protect the Ring from the weak wills of others like Boromir. Uppermost in his mind is the desire to help Middle-earth, if necessary by sacrificing himself for the greater good.

By the end of *Fellowship* Frodo has "grown up" in his acknowledgment of individual autonomy—his freedom to choose. A political hobbit, he also now realizes the threat insiders and friends and desires and fears pose within us all. His future adventures will test his faculties as the drama of the narrative focuses increasingly on differences within both community and self—differences that threaten to divide and disrupt the social and moral order defined by the elven leaders of Rivendell and Lórien. It is name-calling and hostile language, used as a weapon by a friend like Boromir, that wounds more than the compelling words or voice of an enemy like the Black Riders or Sauron. Frodo must now learn how to wield the weapon of language wisely and to recognize its subversive power.

7

Knowledge, Language, and Power: *The Two Towers*

LANGUAGE AND BEING

The Two Towers, as much as any of the three parts of *The Lord of the Rings*, dramatizes the power of language to change, control, dominate—and release. The diminution of intelligent life subverted by its own desires is reflected in the simple baby talk of Gollum to his Ring, his "Precious." And the elevation of intelligent life to supernatural being—the elves—is similarly reflected in their language and song, their ability as Namers, their hold on the past: "Elves made all the old words" (2: 85). Between these two extremes appear other species and types, such as the greedy orcs (like Grishnákh, who is manipulated by the captured Merry's own words, once the hobbit understands the orc's desire) and the long-remembering and all-male ents (like Treebeard, whose memory and thinking powers are considerable). The ents have also (like the elves) composed songs, perhaps more as mnemonic devices than as tributes to history, and have designated certain words to mean ideas (*hill*, for example, is a hasty word for a thing that has stood here for a long time [2: 87]).

The astute reader might well ask, Are the orcs in book 3 merely a deeper echo of Gollum in book 1, broadened into a species inarticulate in its subjugation, divided into warring factions by the opposition between Saruman and Sauron? And are Fangorn and the ents merely an echo of Old Man Willow in the Old Forest? Is

Tolkien intentionally rewriting book 1?

While it is true that we have moved away from the hobbits of the Shire and Buckland and into country ravaged by the conflicts of more powerful warlords, Tolkien is not at an imaginative loss here. The trees of the Old Forest were rooted—and envious of those creatures which could move. The ents *can* move, and in fact have cut off Saruman's escape from Isengard. They are the *leaders* of trees, tree-herds, like shepherds, taught by the elves (2: 89). Their resistance to and rebellion against Saruman is enhanced by his own destruction of the trees—Old Man Willow–like, he hates *living* things and has piecemeal cut down trees of the forest, for he "has a mind of metal and wheels" (2: 96). In fact ents are not exactly trees, or were not. Treebeard tells Merry, "Sheep get like shepherds, and shepherds like sheep, it is said; but slowly, and neither have long in the world. It is quicker and closer with trees and Ents, and they walk down the ages together. For Ents are more like Elves: less interested in themselves than Men are, and better at getting inside other things. And yet again Ents are more like Men, more changeable than Elves are, and quicker at taking the colour of the outside, you might say. Or better than both: for they are steadier and keep their minds on things longer" (2: 89). The ents are one of the four Free Peoples—elf, dwarf, ent and man (2: 84).

The tragedy of the ents is the loss of the entwives. The Ent-wives desired order, plenty, and peace—gardens. In contrast the ents desired wandering, great trees, high woods, and mountain streams. When the Darkness came, gradually the difference between male and female widened until the entwives became only a memory—lost entirely to the ents.

Division and difference in book 1 threatened the harmony of the Shire community, but the threat was diluted by the political skills of Bilbo (and later Frodo), who incarnated those differences in his (their) own temperament. The mating of different Shire families, different types, resulted in progeny whose understanding transcends the limitations of either parent. But for the ents and entwives, regeneration of kind remains an impossibility, and darkness and division mark their history. What the Ents do have is strength—the trolls (made by the Enemy) counterfeit them, as the Enemy also created orcs to counterfeit elves—although, as Treebeard declaims to Merry, "We are stronger than Trolls. We're made of the bones of the earth" (2: 113).

The ents' songs—songs that promised the union of entwives and ents—reflect their withering nature and history, except that, as Treebeard notes, "songs like trees bear fruit only in their own time and their own way: and sometimes they are withered untimely" (2: 114). Intelligent tree-herds, these ents, who incarnate the Idea of Growth that stultifies because its intelligence cannot tolerate female difference. (It is interesting that Tolkien sees cultural and biological differences between male and female ents; in this one specific way he anticipates the French feminist theorists Luce Irigaray, Julia Kristeva, and Hélène Cixous.)

In a sense the ents also project the masculine division between Saruman and Sauron—and the lack of female principle, which Tolkien identifies with the cultivated garden, order, and plenty, as opposed to the wildness of the distant wood, adventure, and distance. It is this female power of healing, growth, and regeneration that Tolkien associates with the creativity of the elves (also to be lost by Middle-earth, like the disappearing entwives) and even, to an extent, in the pastoral Shire. For this reason the emergence of Rose as Sam's wife at the end, in book 6, epitomizes the return of female difference to balance harmoniously with the masculine in the epic's final symbolic "marriage."

Power, so Tolkien insists, must be shared with those individuals and peoples who are different—in gender, nature, history, and temperament. Those who would lead must tolerate difference in expression, latitude, and space rather than choke, ignore, abandon, repress, and kill it. *Rings* is the story of difference articulated, nearly crushed, and only then restored. For Tolkien power involves all that is, has been, and will be, allowed to continue. *Towers*, at the heart of this story, intensifies and explains the nature of difference when domination of one by another is compelled. Let us turn first to book 3.

THE EMPOWERMENT OF THE MARGINALIZED IN BOOK 3

The two strands of the narrative in book 3 (like the two towers of Orthanc and Cirith Ungol in books 5 and 6) symbolize difference and division in the Fellowship and on Middle-earth. Hence the story itself is divided, twin, separated. In the second part—the "upper," or alto or "commanding," part of the narrative (or polyphonic drama)—the "superior" representatives in the Fellowship must look for clues about the missing hobbits Merry and Pippin and also Sam and Frodo (2: 5). Like the entwives, the hobbits are "lost," but in another sense the "lost" hobbits are not so much inferior, unheroic, insignificant (or *different*) as they are, in reality, more important: the little hobbits *are* the story. Tolkien valorizes the marginal and impotent by turning upside down the normal power relationships. Legolas the elf, Gimli the dwarf, and Aragorn the man *must* search for and follow them; it is a humbling and necessary experience. To do so these three must decipher riddles—the signs left by the hobbits to mark their journey. And to detect these signs the three must understand the nature of the hobbits they are following—they must forget themselves and identify with, understand, the hobbit.

One riddle concerns their horses missing in the night (2: 116), startled away with gladness. Another concerns the means by which Merry and Pippin escaped from the orcs (2: 117). Legolas understands that the bound hobbit has escaped from the orcs, cut his bonds with an orc-knife (both bonds and knife remain behind): "But how and why? For if his legs were tied, how did he walk? And if his arms were tied, how did he use the knife? And if neither were tied, why did he cut the cords at all? Being pleased with his skill, he then sat down and quietly ate some waybread! That at least is enough to show that he was a hobbit, without the mallorn-leaf" (2: 117–18). Legolas, though, is not sensitive enough to the ways of hobbits to unravel the entire story. Aragorn also spots orc-blood and hoofprints, thus understanding an orc was killed and hauled away, the hobbit not seen: "But it is a comfort to know that he had some *lembas* in his pocket, even though he ran away without gear or pack; that, perhaps, is like a hobbit" (2: 118). Even Aragorn does not understand why the orcs did not seek out the other members of the company but instead turned away, unless they were commanded to seize live hobbits; he *does* understand the divisive nature of the orc enough to imagine orc treachery for orc ends (2: 19). It is elf and man who are more sensitive to the hobbit nature; Legolas is also sensitive to the dark wood of Fangorn into which the split company must now descend ("Do you not feel the tenseness?" [2: 120], he remarks). And yet even the dwarf Gimli has learned to accept this wood-elf ("though Elves of any kind are strange folk" [2: 120]) and the comfort he offers him: "Where you go, I will go." It is a strange marriage of opposites, this fellowship, and yet it epitomizes the United Nations, which must eventually allow all different nations to coexist in peace in Middle-earth's coming Fourth Age, of man.

The reader must also "track" their progress—the characters now command the attention of their reader, again subverting the hierarchical power relationship a less skillful author might imagine inheres in the artistic process, for art does consist of signs, riddles, and clues, which the perceptive tracker pieces together (and which that "tracker" could shut down merely by closing the book). Help is provided by Gandalf the Grey, who (deus ex machina–like) reemerges here as Mithrandir—the White (2: 125).

Note that Gandalf speaks in "riddles": "No! For I was talking aloud to myself. A habit of the old: they choose the wisest person present to speak to; the long explanations needed by the young are wearying" (2: 127). Gandalf's clarification to Aragorn spells out Tolkien's concept of knowledge of difference as power, to be used successfully by the Fellowship until the ultimate moment in this story. Gandalf the White acknowledges that Sauron understands the Ring is carried by a hobbit and attended by a Fellowship, but because Sauron is limited by his own desire, his own self (read: selfishness), he does not understand the nature and motivations of his adversary, so different from Sauron. Gandalf explains: "He supposes that we were all going to Minas Tirith; for that is what he would himself have done in our place. And according to his wisdom it would have been a heavy stroke against his power. Indeed he is in great fear, not knowing what mighty one may suddenly appear, wielding the Ring, and assailing him with war, seeking to cast him down and take his place. That we should wish to cast him down and have *no* one in his place is not a thought that occurs to his mind. That we should try to destroy the Ring itself has not yet entered into his darkest dream" (2: 127).

Because of his inability to think as a non-power-seeking hobbit would, Sauron does not guard carefully enough the borders of his own Mordor. He lacks the imagination that propels the small hobbit to take the offensive—"attacking" Mordor by destroying the one object that could guarantee the diminutive being's power.

Furthermore, the divisiveness of the Dark Community has erupted into the treachery of Saruman against his own Master, a rebellion fueled by a Sauron-like greed for the domination and power afforded by possession of the Ring. And thus Saruman similarly does not understand hobbit difference enough to use that knowledge as power. In his desire for the Ring, Saruman has plotted to capture Merry and Pippin, which has only brought them more efficiently and quickly to Fangorn—in accord with the company's quest. Gandalf comments on Saruman's inability to perceive difference, both of hobbit and of tree: "He does not yet know his peril. There is much that he does not know. I look into his mind and I see his doubt. He has no woodcraft. He believes that the horsemen slew and burned all upon the field of battle; but he does not know whether the Orcs were bringing any prisoners or not. And he does not know of the quarrel between his servants and the Orcs of Mordor; nor does he know of the Winged Messenger" (2: 129). Unfortunately, Saruman must have the Ring in order to battle Mordor, and he will not have it; he also fights Rohan, and he does not suspect that the ents will unite to destroy *him* and his axes as Saruman has attempted to destroy *them* one by one.

That the company was not sure whether the obscure figure they saw was Gandalf or Saruman pinpoints the ambiguity of signs and the difficulty in "reading" (meaning *understanding*) correctly. Gandalf *does* know the answer to this and many other questions, which makes him dangerous. He also knows that the path to victory passes through death and despair—a path the company must choose on its own, emulating the metamorphosis of Gandalf as the White. In fighting the Balrog ("In that despair my enemy was my only hope" [2: 134]) so that Gandalf brought him to the Endless Stair, the wizard threw down his enemy, who broke the mountainside. (Thereafter Gandalf entered darkness wandering, and was sent back naked and forgotten, until the Windlord took him again to Lothlórien to be healed [2: 134–35]). Accordingly, the company members learn from those elves the way of *their* victory:

Near is the hour when the Lost should come forth,
And the Grey Company ride from the North.
But dark is the path appointed for thee:
The Dead watch the road that leads to the Sea.

(2: 136)

What Gandalf means is that his enemy's knowledge (in lieu of his own) provides his only hope of survival, in that the Balrog will attempt to save himself, and therein lies Gandalf's survival. Because his situation is so hopeless, he must trust in his adversary's knowledge, which gives him power. Thus he advises the company, and in particular Aragorn, that *their* hope lies paradoxically in a path through despair; that their lives can be preserved only through death; and that their future exists only insofar as they acknowledge the mistakes of the past—that is, in the restorative aid of the Dead Company, a foil for them.

From here on in book 3 of *Towers* the message that knowledge—language—confers power and that the road to hope passes through despair is parlayed in various dramatic reenactments of the previous scene. Théoden emerges as a wise leader from the despair successfully wrought by Wormtongue's self-serving and critical words; Saruman as a fallen leader refuses all hope in the prison of Orthanc he has created for himself out of incomplete knowledge. That Wormtongue the bad servant will, by the novel's end, become the ignominious servant "Worm" of the snarling "Sharkey" (or Saruman)—also bad servant, of Sauron—seems entirely logical and appropriate. That Rohan and Isengard as places that they control are exchanged for the more humble Shire by the trilogy's end mirrors their epic devolution as their cleverness diminishes into wordless animality ("*Worm,*" "*Sharkey*") to signal their moral and natural deterioration. That both will help finance the disgusting Lotho Sackville-Baggins in his apparent rise to power back at the Shire returns us to the beginning of *Rings*, in "The Birthday Party." In Tolkien, Worm *is* a worm and Sharkey *is* a shark—the word for the thing, the name, always reflects its true nature. These two major confrontations show us how.

In Rohan (chapter 6) the reader (like the company) confronts the recently erected chauvinistic barrier of language: "It is the will of Théoden King that none should enter his gates, save those who know our tongue and are our friends" (2: 143), the guard replies when Gandalf asks why they do not speak in the Common Tongue. (It was not always so in Rohan, we learn later [2: 160].) The assumption is that their own folk will speak their own tongue and thus will pose no threat to their tribe. And yet it is Wormtongue who has imposed this literalistic and superficial barrier to ingress—Wormtongue, the traitor working close to the throne for Saruman (himself a traitor in the "House" of Sauron). In a similar literalism the hall guardians demand that the weapons of the company be left outside the hall (2: 144), an ironic gesture, given the debilitating ruin of king and country wrought not by sword but by tongue, and words, of the king's counselor who encourages him to eat and rest rather than to fight and rule (2: 157). Aragorn counters the edict of Rohan with a similar spell as he unbuckles the Blade that was Broken: "Here I set it . . . but I command you not to touch it, nor to permit any other to lay hand on it. . . . Death shall come to any man that draws Elendil's sword save Elendil's heir" (2: 147). Words here muster greater power than swords, and *past* words—history—muster greater power than do present words. And so the guard responds admiringly to Aragorn, "It seems that you are come on the wings of *song* out of the forgotten days" (2: 147; my italics).

The conflict is one of wills, and of the wills of two kings, rather than of swords per se. Théoden is (supposedly) king in his own hall, but Aragorn, king of all men. Who is to say Aragorn *is* the rightful king to whom even Théoden owes allegiance? And who is to say the staff on which Gandalf leans is an old man's stick or a wizard's wand? Háma the hall guardian ultimately allows Gandalf to pass *with* staff in hand because "in doubt a man of worth will trust to his own wisdom. I believe you are friends and folk worthy of honour, who have no evil purpose" (2: 147). Perhaps Háma has long realized that the "king" in his own hall is ruled by his counselor Wormtongue.

To expose vulnerability (whether of nation or of person) to another means letting down barriers both literal and figurative; Wormtongue has operated and operates now by working on Théoden's fear. Wormtongue reiterates the "bitter tidings" preceding the arrival of "Gandalf Stormcrow"—the death in battle of Théodred, Théoden's son, and the stirrings of the Dark Lord in the East (2: 149). Wormtongue even inverts Adam's creative role as Namer (or the Middle-earth equivalent, the elven role of naming) in churlishly calling Gandalf *Láthspell,* "Ill-news" (2: 149). Furthermore, Wormtongue denigrates the wizard's present mission through a reminder of the past mission to Rohan, along the way discrediting Gandalf's followers as "Three ragged wanderers in grey, and you yourself the most beggar-like of the four!" (2: 150). The bringer of ill tidings must himself be evil, and so Wormtongue's skewed and rude logic instructs Théoden, just as the wearer of ragged clothing must himself be a beggar in need of aid.

Gandalf's lesson to Wormtongue (and Théoden and Rohan) reveals clearly that appearances may mask a higher reality—a lesson in symbolism *and* courtesy. The appearances of the three followers belie their regal identity, as Elendil's heir, elf, and dwarf. Moreover, Gandalf reveals that they are clad in humble raiment because the elves bestowed that gray clothing on them. But this bestowal is falsely termed by Wormtongue an alliance with the deceptive, web-weaving "Sorceress of the Golden Wood" (2: 150).

Gandalf then, snakelike, sheds his false outer appearance of the weak old man, dependent on staff, to sing of Galadriel without stain—that is, to reveal the truth, to put on the new person: "The wise speak only of what they know, Gríma son of Gálmód. A witless worm have you become. Therefore be silent, and keep your forked tongue behind your teeth. I have not passed through fire and death to bandy crooked words with a serving-man till the lightning falls" (2: 151). Wormtongue twists words and meanings to serve his own purpose—and that of Saruman—but it is not the purpose of truth or of Rohan. Furthermore, Wormtongue's counsel to Théoden has heightened the fear of the old king in order to subvert Théoden's sovereign role to that of the "serving-man," Wormtongue.

Gandalf's rescue alerts Théoden to light instead of dark, to hope instead of despair, by means of encouraging instead of critical and destructive words (Wormtongue has scolded Théoden, "Did I not counsel you, lord, to forbid his staff? That fool, Háma, has betrayed us!" [2: 151], criticizing both Théoden's folly in not listening to Wormtongue and Háma's folly). What exactly does Gandalf say to evoke change in Théoden that restores him to his rightful place as sovereign? Only to urge *optimism*—courage and wisdom—in a respectful manner. Gandalf declares, "Not all is dark. Take courage, Lord of the Mark; for better help you will not find. No counsel have I to give to those that despair. Yet counsel I could give, and words I could speak to you. Will you hear them? They are not for all ears. I bid you come out before your doors and look abroad. Too long have you sat in shadows and trusted to twisted tales and crooked promptings" (2: 151).

In short, the suspicions and fears of the hall guardian—and the resistance to differences in language and nationality—reflect the darkness within the tribe and its king, the despair to which all (save Éomer) have succumbed when heeding critical and punitive words. Who can one trust, if all are untrustworthy? Who can one trust, if one remains safely incarcerated indoors, too old to venture out into danger? Who can one trust if one cannot trust oneself? Yet the chief danger to Rohan all along has come from *within*, from that familiar sameness mistaken as loving and protective—Wormtongue. Once again Tolkien trumpets forth the power of language to destroy and manipulate—or to recuperate and restore. Once again real knowledge depends on a recognition of good beneath superficial difference and seemingly humble appearance.

Facing fear rather than evading it (or protecting against it) and conquering self-pity become Gandalf's counsel once again. As he and Théoden face Mordor, the wizard announces, "that way lies our hope [read: Frodo and Sam], where sits our greatest fear [read: Sauron]. Doom hangs still on a thread. Yet hope there is still, if we can but stand unconquered for a little while [read: to buy extra time for Frodo and Sam to return the Ring safely]" (2: 154). And when Théoden complains of war and evil in that old age he had imagined as deserving peace, while the "young perish and the old linger," Gandalf reminds him that he no longer wears a sword: "Your fingers would remember their old strength better, if they grasped a sword-hilt" (2: 154). He reminds the king, in short, that kings are kings, whatever their age, because they command in battle and rule. The sword is a symbol of power, both physical and political; to deprive a king of his sword is to deny him his rightful role, to diminish his power. Thus the converse is true: to return a sword is to acknowledge and respect strength. This the true servant Éomer does: "As his [Théoden's] fingers took the hilt, it seemed to the watchers that firmness and strength returned to his thin arm. Suddenly he lifted the blade and swung it shimmering and whistling in the air. Then he gave a great cry. . . . 'Arise now, arise,

Riders of Théoden!'" (2: 155). Trust becomes the operative word of counsel.

Indeed, when Théoden "trusts" that Wormtongue will accompany him to battle, the true cowardice of the false servant stands exposed. The choice Wormtongue makes reveals his own weak and untrustworthy nature—to stay behind in safety or, if that is not possible, to return to Saruman. Wormtongue's literalism sees Théoden as old, incapable: "But those who truly love him would spare his failing year" (2: 158). He fails to understand that love means respect for inner capability—leadership—despite the outer limits of physical strength. Gandalf shows all that which Wormtongue subverts in order to win Éowyn as his prize (2: 159). This is the worm's true goal, this Satan-like seduction of Théoden. The soothing and appealing words of the Snake tempt more, perhaps, but as Théoden acknowledges later of his true servant Éomer, "Faithful heart may have froward tongue" (2: 161).

The tribe of Rohan convinces us that the old may be stronger than their appearance suggests; so also we will learn later that the most valorous warrior may indeed be female rather than male. Éowyn, daughter of Éomund, will serve Rohan in battle better than any other Rider from the Mark. She is also awarded lordship of Rohan in their absence. Throughout, ignominious hobbits, the frail elderly, and the female occupy for Tolkien the most heroic roles. It is interesting to note, given Háma's previous "folly" in admitting the ragged company with Gandalf's staff, that Háma the hall guardian offers Théoden the advice to make Éowyn lord. Háma's wisdom sees beneath surface difference—a facility that makes him an invaluable counselor and a trustworthy "reader" of the text of human character.

THE DEFEAT OF THE DEHUMANIZED IN BOOK 3

The second locus in which knowledge, language, and power emerge as central to victory in a dramatic battle occurs not so much at the literal battle of Helm's Deep as at the final meeting at Orthanc, the palace of Saruman that becomes his prison. There too the battle is one of words, one in which Gandalf again functions as a principal, to overcome Saruman as a far more cunning adversary than Wormtongue. Like Grishnákh and later Wormtongue, Saruman is a traitor—to the White Council he supposedly leads. As Wormtongue serves Saruman, so Saruman, by reading the *palantír*, inadvertently and unknowingly serves Sauron, who controls its visions and hence knows its users.

Of the two towers of this second volume, one belongs to Saruman's Orthanc and the other to Shelob's Cirith Ungol. And yet even in book 3 the way to that first tower is through the hall of Rohan, where the servant of Saruman has attempted to destroy king and nation. Wormtongue even in the Shire will kill his leader after a final verbal abuse—the traitor will once again betray his own "master." In the second half of *Towers* Gollum functions with Frodo as a type of Wormtongue to Théoden in the service *he* provides, ultimately betraying them to Shelob (Saruman's counterpart in this second half) as Rohan has been betrayed to Saruman.

Saruman, then, and the spider Shelob (Sauron's "cat") represent two monstrous "servants" to Sauron. Their two towers project forth their differing powers. "Orthanc" (or Mount Fang, "Cunning Mind") celebrates in its iconology the intellectual perversion of Saruman just as "Cirith Ungol" ("Pass of the Spider") typifies in its dramatic purpose (the capture of prey) the physical horror embodied in the greedy Shelob.

Saruman's particular gift has always been his ingenuity, a wizard knowledge set to the capitalist's profit motive at whatever the cost. Accordingly, he has interbred orcs with goblin men to withstand the coming of the sun and therefore to fight successfully during the day (2: 180). This entrepreneur has also enlisted the hate of the wild men of the hills for the men of Gondor and Rohan in the battle against Aragorn and his company. Saruman's technological mind has sought the wasting of forests and Nan Curunír (the Wizard's Vale), where Isengard is located, to power his factories, smithies, and furnaces. And so Saruman exploits the labor of slaves, and the dark architectonics of Orthanc and wasteland in the once-green valley clarify his self-aggrandizing purpose: riches and power.

For example, Orthanc is surrounded by one protective, great ring-wall of stone ("like towering cliffs" [2: 203]), perhaps to suggest to the reader its similarity to the one controlling Ring. Only one entrance is carved into the southern wall, and it leads to a tunnel stopped at both ends by iron doors. That the ingenuity of Saruman has been employed to increase the efficiency of his instruments of imprisonment and empowerment is reflected in the excellence of these iron doors: "They were so wrought and poised upon their huge hinges, posts of steel driven into the living stone, that when unbarred they could be moved with a light thrust of the arms, noiselessly" (2: 203). Saruman has exchanged the green, fruitful, bowl-shaped plain within the wall for dark stone flags and for chained marble and metal pillars marching in columns. The many houses cut into the walls overlooking the open circle resemble a honeycomb; the plain too has been "bored and delved. Shafts were driven deep into the ground; their ends were covered by low mounds and domes of stone, so that in the moonlight the Ring of Isengard looked like a graveyard of unquiet dead" (2: 203). Iron wheels revolve; night vapors steam. All roads run to the center of Isengard, where the black rock tower of Orthanc in its construction also mirrors the complexity and violent wickedness of Saruman's own cunning mind, even though the tower was made not by him but by "builders of old" ("yet it seemed a thing not made by the craft of Man, but riven from the bones of the earth in the ancient torment of the hills" [2: 204]). Saruman rapes Middle-earth in his painful acquisitive progression toward power, and the violence of his desire matches the "gaping horns" at the top of Orthanc, "their pinnacles sharp as the points of spears, keen-edged as knives" (2: 204).

Saruman's specific contribution to Orthanc—once beautiful and always strong, the residence of great lords and astrologers, or Magi (2: 204)—has been its reshaping to what he imagines are his own purposes: "and made it better, as he thought, being deceived—for all those arts and subtle devices, for which he forsook his former wisdom, and which fondly he imagined were his own, came but from Mordor" (2: 204). His creativity, then, is a blank, a zero, nothing—a mirror imitation of that destructivity typical of the power of Sauron: "What he made was naught, only a little copy, a child's model or a slave's flattery, of that vast fortress, armoury, prison, furnace of great power, Barad-dûr, the Dark Tower, which suffered no rival, and laughed at flattery, biding its time, secure in its pride and its immeasurable strength" (2: 204).

What destroys the doors of Isengard is the "Great Sea" that fills the "bowl" of the plain of Isengard and isolates the single tower of Orthanc. The River Isen has been dammed up by the furious ents in order to flood Isengard's tunnel and thus overwhelm the city. Appropriately, the tree-killer Saruman is overcome by trees—and the rocks of Isengard torn asunder by the root-splitting power of the victimized. Of course the ents and huorns cannot best a wizard, but the elemental antagonism ("Wood and water, stock and stone" [2: 223]) is fulfilled by their united efforts: "Isengard looked like a huge flat saucepan, all steaming and bubbling" (2: 225). What gets "cooked" is of course Saruman.

We might add to Tolkien's empowerment of marginalized peoples and societies the trees—and their ents and huorns. The exploited helpless—whether aged, female, childlike, or even plant-like in nature—are urged into heroism and action throughout. Even the childlike (and seemingly superfluous) Merry and Pippin in their separate adventure with orcs and ents assume new identities after a heroic metamorphosis into door-wardens: Merry introduces himself as Meriadoc, son of Saradoc; Pippin, as Peregrin, son of Paladin, "of the house of Took" (2: 206). We relive the encounter of the Split Company and Háma at the door to the palace in Rohan. The hobbits prove able enough to withstand the patronizing and frustrated diatribes of Gimli and Legolas as they scold the little fellows for their childish truancy ("You rascals, you woolly-footed and wool-pated truants!" [2: 207], Gimli cries). It is Pippin who responds drily, "One thing you have not found in your hunting, and that's brighter wits" (2: 207). Even the company finds itself at odds, the greater and stronger treating the smaller and weaker as literally as do Háma and Wormtongue in the earlier encounter.

Here Théoden is offered the opportunity to greet them with the real authority of a wise leader, and he does. When he learns these are hobbits—which he first identifies by the name he knows best, "Holbytlan"—he is corrected by Pippin ("Hobbits, if you please, lord"), and he courteously respects both their language (so different from his) and their otherness by symbolically bowing to them: "No report that I had heard does justice to the truth" (2: 207). There is majesty in graciousness and humility, in respect for the Other, Tolkien seems to say. Where Gimli and Legolas fail, at least mildly repeating the errors of Wormtongue, Théoden succeeds well. Even when Théoden acknowledges of the hobbits that "there are no legends of their deeds, for it is said that they do little" (2: 208), he never uses this hearsay to denigrate them: "But it seems that more could be said" (2: 208). Trust and openness, toleration and good manners—all are qualities necessary in the politic leader Théoden epitomizes.

The meeting between Saruman and Gandalf, however, operates on a different level. Saruman holds power—has held power —because of his voice (as chapter 10 reminds us, "The Voice of Saruman"). "Wormtongue" as a name has hinted at the ability of Grima to twist language and words to seductive ends (e.g., urging Théoden to eat and rest rather than to fight and lead—words of counsel that only at first glance seem thoughtful and solicitous of the king's welfare). Saruman's eloquence far exceeds Wormtongue's because it springs from wizard cunning masked by kindness and graciousness (all those qualities that the good king Théoden has so amply demonstrated). The difference is that his voice seems to be separate from his actions—what he says and what he does are twin, dual: "Suddenly another voice spoke, low and melodious, its very sound an enchantment. Those who listened unwarily to that voice could seldom report the words that they heard; and if they did, they wondered, for little power remained in them. Mostly they remembered only that it was a delight to hear the voice speaking, all that it said seemed wise and reasonable" (2: 234).

The voice (and note how disembodied and dehumanized Tolkien imagines it) is evil because its beauty arouses the envy of its listeners: "desire awoke in them by swift agreement to seem wise themselves" (2: 234). The wizard's spell works to seduce them into his power because it makes all other voices (especially voices raised in disagreement) seem "harsh and uncouth" and it arouses the listeners' anger. It seduces by arousing the listener's admiration for the speaker, who seems so bent on helping and understanding the listener. When Saruman addresses Théoden ("O worthy son of Thengel the Thrice-renowned!" [2: 235]), not only does he employ flattery and rhetoric to convince the king ("mightiest king of western lands") of his desire to aid him in his hour of need—which is what we all *want* to hear ("Why have you not come before, and as a friend?" [2: 25])—but he also deliberately lies and intimidates through fear ("still I would save you, and deliver you from the ruin that draws nigh inevitably, if you ride upon this road which you have taken. Indeed I alone can aid you now" [2: 234]). The courtesy and respect imbuing his speech seem appropriate to the stature of the king he addresses; the fear of which he reminds the men of Rohan is omnipresent and all too powerful: "And over their hearts crept a shadow, the fear of a great danger: the end of the Mark in a darkness to which Gandalf was driving them, while Saruman stood beside a door of escape, holding it half open so that a ray of light came through" (2: 235).

Desire and fear, the twin weapons of the orator, seem as nothing before the level and plain truth, but that is what both Gimli the dwarf (the species closest to earth) and Éomer the good servant, who formerly offended by speaking unwelcome words, offer in retaliation. The first reminds the company and Rohan that Orthanc's language always speaks in reverse: "The words of this wizard stand on their heads. . . . In the language of Orthanc help means ruin, and saving means slaying, that is plain. But we do not come here to beg" (2: 235). The second reminds Théoden of the present situation and the treachery of this "old liar with honey on his forked tongue" (2: 236). It is Saruman who is the "trapped wolf," not they. Théoden chooses the honesty of common folk and speaks plainly himself: "Harsh as an old raven's their master's voice sounded in their ears after the music of Saruman" (2: 237). And Théoden's refusal to acquiesce leads to Saruman's hissing metamorphosis into snakelike negativity and crushing belittlement ("Dotard!" he then calls Théoden).

Saruman's pride plumes up himself and enforces this diminution of all others—of Otherness. To the proud all outside the Self *is* Other, Different. And so Saruman then appeals to Gandalf in what seems "the gentle remonstrance of a kindly king with an erring but much-loved minister. But they were shut out, listening at a door to words not meant for them: ill-mannered children or stupid servants overhearing the elusive discourse of their elders" (2: 238–39). Gandalf laughs, however, and asks him only to come down—that is, to humble himself as well as to literally step down from the tower—and thereby admit his error and save himself. The monster that Saruman has become refuses, and Gandalf, now the White and superior in the Council to Saruman, casts him out of both the order of wizards and from the Council (2: 241). "He will not serve, only command" (2: 242) is Gandalf's accurate assessment. But Gandalf will do nothing to him, because he does not long for mastery and because "Often does hatred hurt itself" (2: 243).

The last contest in book 3 belongs to Pippin and Sauron, through the *palantír* held by Saruman until Wormtongue heaves it down near his head. The temptation to look into "that which looks far away" (2: 258), especially because Pippin has touched it, provokes the most unlikely contest, that between hobbit and Dark Lord (2: 252). The *palantír* has a magical power like that of the Ring; that Pippin succumbs (as Frodo does to the Ring at the end of *Fellowship*) is no surprise. And yet the seeming crushing loss to Sauron (for Pippin faints in terror after his "interrogation") is actually a victory: Sauron's assumption is that this hobbit is imprisoned in Orthanc by Saruman, and thus the Red Eye will lose precious time because of this error, for the real Ringbearer is nearing Mordor. Once again literalism, ignorance, and pride reduce power; once again a marginalized protagonist succeeds.

Humility in Tolkien is always ultimately successful, especially in this case, as it has saved Middle-earth: had Gandalf been tempted to look within, he might have lost the battle with Sauron (2: 255). How appropriate that the greatest wizard is rescued from the possibility of his own subversion by the least of hobbits. The power of humility and ignominy, and of language (again symbolized by the visionary *palantír*), will be extended and deepened in the next book, in which the stage is further reduced to an even more crucial hobbit level.

THE ARTICULATE BODY IN BOOK 4

Isengard and Mordor have managed to communicate by means of the *palantír* that links Sauron and his "servant" Saruman. The link between books 3 and 4 of *Rings* is provided by the two towers of Sauron's "servant" Saruman and his "cat" Shelob. This political theme of good, and good service, unifies the whole of *Towers* as the dehumanization of culture and civilizations darkens into the increasingly interiorized drama of Sam and Frodo, servant and master, in the fourth book. More insistently now, Tolkien will ask,

How knowledge, if no language? What power is conferred in the absence of language, at that moment when speechlessness, silence, or unpatterned sound, crosses into the bestiality of a Shelob? When Sam and Frodo leave the "Window on the West" in book 4, "all about them was silence. The birds seemed all to have flown away or to have fallen dumb" (2: 386). What is the significant difference between the dehumanization of a wise wizard and the privileging of the cruel and predatory greed of a powerful giant spider? In what ways is uncontrolled irrationality (Shelob) more dangerous than uncontrolled cunning (Saruman)? Is uncontrolled irrationality even conscious of difference in the way we have been defining it? Can degeneration and reification be undone, moral consciousness retrieved?

In the East, Mordor is named after the Anglo-Saxon word for "murder." Accordingly, the land it names conveys the idea of death, violence, extinction of the Other. The separation between Self and Other suggests difference; a wise leader will acknowledge and respect differences in order to attract followers. In Mordor, there is no such thing as separation of Self from Other: difference is consumed, swallowed up, by the Self. It is this particularly monstrous and uncivilized tyranny that Shelob represents. Here death means the murder of the Other and therefore the unnatural insistence upon the Self at the expense of the Other. It is no coincidence that, as Frodo and Sam trek through the dead lands, the "wind was chilly and yet heavy with an odor of cold decay" (2: 266). Frodo's ironic heroism demands that he move slowly if inexorably toward self-sacrifice—and the Shadow that threatens to extinguish him *and* the Ring.

Gollum, who follows these "thieves" in the hopes of recuperating his Precious, hates them (2: 280), his very hate the seed of murder (Mordor). And yet in his incarnation of the death of Other symbolized by Mordor, he reveals the isolation of the Self that must destroy or assimilate the Other in order to survive. In a telling incident in "The Taming of Sméagol" (chapter 1) Frodo once again has the opportunity to kill Gollum, who has tracked Frodo and Sam to their hiding place near a precipice. Gollum, however, pleads for mercy, identifying himself as the prey of the "cats" (2: 280; Frodo and Sam?) and therefore foreshadowing the later attack on Frodo by the far-larger and more predatory "cat" of Sauron, Shelob. His reason for clemency is his loneliness, his isolation, or—given the seeming singleness of his identity—his nature as difference person-ified. He is unique, he is one, and in his grotesque singleness, his Otherness, he desires companionship—the acknowledgment that difference is meaningless: "They won't hurt us will they, nice little hobbitses? We didn't mean no harm, but they jumps on us like cats on poor mices, they did, precious. And we're so lonely, *gollum.* We'll be nice to them, very nice, if they'll be nice to us, want us, yes, yess" (2: 280).

The incident also reminds Frodo of his earlier reaction to Gan-dalf's recounting of the meeting of Bilbo and Gollum, when Bilbo's pity stayed his hand. At the time Frodo's indignation denied him mercy, and yet at this moment, now that Frodo "sees" (read: under-stands) Gollum, he *does* in fact pity the degenerate hobbit (2: 281). Frodo's pity urges him to reach out to that tiny speck of hobbit, of grace, of nonbestiality, still inherent in Gollum's nature, that which separates the nearly inarticulate ("Gollum," a gulp) from the bestial (such as Shelob). And so Frodo *respects* Gollum's difference and appeals to their common denominator of hobbitness by addressing the creature, not by the humiliating and degrading (if accurate) name Gollum but by the original and untarnished name Sméagol (2: 283). Frodo also tells him the truth—another gesture of respect: they *are* headed for Mordor. What Frodo and Gollum share, it appears, is a desire to prevent the Ring ("Precious") from falling into the power of Sauron. This desire unites them in a common goal: safe passage through the Dead Marshes.

Gollum initially refuses this respect for his difference, appar-ently preferring his present nonself: "Don't ask Sméagol. Poor, poor Sméagol, he went away long ago. They took his Precious, and he's lost now" (2: 283). He prefers the easier state of annihilation of con-sciousness, past, and self in which he exists as Gollum, the name for a sound made when swallowing, like that made when speaking or eating. Frodo offers him the hope of the recovery of self: "Perhaps we'll find him again, if you come with us" (2: 283). Frodo treats Gollum-Sméagol as Théoden does Pippin, with respect and cour-tesy, and he similarly provides leadership by offering encourage-ment, hope, and praise. Like Théoden, he is motivated by pity, mercy, and love. This arouses in both Pippin and Gollum a latent and grateful desire to serve.

The ceremony of investiture performed on Gollum by Frodo
(2: 285) invites the doglike Gollum to swear by the Precious to
freely do what the lordly Frodo wishes, to be "very very good" and to
never let "Him" have the Ring. The feudal relationship between
them here seems to heighten their difference: "For a moment it
appeared to Sam that his master had grown and Gollum had
shrunk: a tall stern shadow, a mighty lord who hid his brightness
in grey cloud, and at his feet a little whining dog" (2: 285). Ironically
Gollum will keep his promise to Frodo until he bites off his lord's
ring finger. This bite (a final *gollum*?) serves all far better than he
knows and even in treachery enables a rescue of Middle-earth that
leads to Gollum's own annihilation. Hobbit Frodo and former hobbit
Sméagol are, however, more same than different at this instant of
mutual identification in book 3: "Yet the two were in some way akin
and not alien: they could reach one another's minds" (2: 285). Their
kinship presupposes Gollum *has* a mind to reach. Gollum has been
raised to consciousness and premeditation by a ceremony resem-
bling that of a wedding in its union of opposites—of course one not
marked by difference in gender, class, or race but by difference in
moral values. After this event Gollum whines and hisses less and is
more eager to please because he is now more Other-directed: "He
spoke to his companions direct, not to his precious self. . . . He
would cackle with laughter and caper if any jest was made, or even
if Frodo spoke kindly to him, and weep if Frodo rebuked him"
(2: 286). It is Frodo's words of acceptance that catalyze this change
in Gollum-Sméagol.

In book 4 the symbolic settings developing these ideas appear
in the Dead Marshes, the Garden of Gondor where Frodo, Sam and
Gollum encounter Faramir the Steward, brother to the dead
Boromir, and Cirith Ungol. Betrayal and service become polar
extremes on a political continuum that ultimately inverts itself: betrayal can in reality be service, just as service (as we have learned
in book 3 through Grishnákh, Wormtongue, and Saruman) can in
reality be betrayal. Who is to decide what service is, who is to
decide what betrayal is—who knows absolutely? Does Gollum in
actuality betray Frodo? Does Frodo fail to protect his servant Gollum? And when at the end Master Samwise must make hard
choices as Ringbearer, does he choose out of wisdom or out of
vengeance? Who is master, who servant?

Gollum's metamorphosis is marked by a kind of primitive, body-directed song:

> The cold hard lands
> they bites our hands,
> they gnaws our feet.
> The rocks and stones
> are like old bones
> all bare of meat.
>
> (2: 287–88)

That food imagery surfaces in his composition reflects Gollum's obsessions and—as Sam puts it—in general what heroic narrative rarely describes, "the problem of food" (2: 288). Can heroism continue if the body is not fed? Sam later quotes his father: "Where there's life there's hope . . . *and need of vittles*" (2: 392). Gollum also sings a riddle about catching a fish ("never thirsting, ever drinking; clad in mail, never clinking" [2: 288]). Food, we recall, has always been the hobbit's passion. A hobbit being compelled into a heroic mode, being denied his passion, and having his survival depend on the knowledge of an unhobbit in whom he must trust is a most unnatural situation.

The Dead Marshes (east of the Emyn Muil) included graves of men and elves, killed during the Battle of Dagorlad, "when Sméagol was young" (2: 297); along with orcs they peer out from the water when candles are lit: "They lie in all the pools, pale faces, deep deep under the dark water. I saw them: grim faces and evil, and noble faces and sad. Many faces proud and fair, and weeds in their silver hair. But all foul, all rotting, all dead" (2: 297). This mockery of the Last Alliance (read: representatives of all races united in a common purpose at death) signifies the past failure to resist Sauron. The Marshes thus symbolize death and despair (*Mordor*) and act as a psychological deterrent to the Fellowship's progress: to move forward they must conquer their own aversion to death and failure, their lack of hope at the possibility of succeeding, the ultimate futility of their mission. How can mere hobbits succeed against Sauron when led by a treacherous creature like Gollum and when so many have failed in the past?

What keeps them going is that they are attempting not to battle Sauron—to test him in physical combat—but merely to return the

Ring to its source. Still, the despair and darkness take their toll on all of them, especially Gollum (who has been captured once before and who is terrified of the Dark Lord) and Frodo (whose Ringbearing wearies him to exhaustion—"He was now beginning to feel it as an actual weight dragging him earthwards" [2: 300]—and whose awareness of the gaze of the other stultifies him). It is the latter awareness that he must resist even more than the former, a resistance to being seen, reified, petrified: "The Eye: that horrible growing sense of a hostile will that strove with great power to pierce all shadows of cloud, and earth, and flesh, and to see you: to pin you under its deadly gaze, naked, immovable. So thin, so frail and thin, the veils were become that still warded it off" (2: 301).

The Eye is not yet aware of where Frodo is, but he can sense its ever-searching power, Medusa-like in its ability to paralyze. (It epitomizes the criticism directed at the Other, the different: the gaze is one of hostility, wrath, death, annihilation.) For Gollum "lust of the Ring that was so near" counters the "pressure of the Eye" and conflicts with the promise to guide them that he has made to Frodo (2: 301). Only Sam does not notice the "dark cloud that had fallen on his own heart," so concerned is he with Frodo. The pressure of darkness brings to the fore latent desire and fear: in passing through the Dead Marshes the company must struggle with its own dark emotions, the worst of which is despair. Even once past, the land they encounter is a wasteland ("gasping pools . . . choked with ash and crawling muds, sickly white and grey, as if the mountains had vomited the filth of their entrails upon the lands about . . . like an obscene graveyard in endless rows . . . a land defiled, diseased beyond all healing" [2: 302]).

The paramount desolation of the land mirrors the desolation of Gollum's soul: we are exploring the symbolic landscape of degenerate and blasted intelligence; can moral choices be made at all in the face of such absolute devastation and nothingness? The drama of Gollum-Sméagol is played out in a soul debate in which the Promise vies with the desire for the Ring, liking and respect for Frodo with hatred for Bilbo (who "stole" the Ring) and for Sam ("the nasty suspicious hobbit" [2: 304]), all intermingled with fear of Sauron.

The way out—the *moral* way out, for an immoral being caught between impossible pressures—is to deny culpability for desire by transferring responsibility to some other agency—Shelob in this case ("She might help" [2: 305]). If the giant spider kills the hobbits, then Gollum is free to snitch the Ring and he has not in fact broken his literal Promise to Frodo. This logic involves a neat sidestepping of the moral issue—a means of lessening intolerable pressure through rationalization.

The pressure increases when they discover that Cirith Gorgor, the Haunted Pass where the Teeth (or Towers) of Mordor stand watch, is fully guarded (2: 308). This unfortunate circumstance tightens the screws for Gollum too, once he understands the firmness of Frodo's resolve to continue onward: Gollum does wish to serve his Master; he *has* brought them to the Gate, as Frodo has requested; he does *not* wish the Ring to fall into Sauron's hands; and by obeying Frodo he disobeys Sauron, whom he fears and hates. The path Gollum suggests is the path of least resistance, into Shelob's lair (read: the way of rationalization). Does Gollum deceive Frodo by offering him this alternative, or does he aid him?

Frodo uses the only weapon he has against such easy moral evasion: the harsh clarity of truth. In his foreshadowing the end of *Rings*, Frodo paints clearly the consequences of Gollum's desire for the Ring: "You will never get it back. In the last need, Sméagol, I should put on the Precious; and the Precious mastered you long ago. If I, wearing it, were to command you, you would obey, even if it were to leap from a precipice or to cast yourself into the fire. And such would be my command" (2: 314). At the end Gollum so desires the Ring that he obeys when Frodo apparently commands him to leap into the precipice, *but*, equally, the Precious ultimately also masters Frodo. Thus Gollum's final desire (and treachery) indeed represents a final service—to the Precious *and* to his Master Frodo. If both master and servant "fail" against the power of the Ring, their matched failures nevertheless balance against the fate of Middle-earth: the Free Peoples are saved. Gollum's biting of the ring finger repeats history, given Isildur's cutting of Sauron's finger in the past.

The Tower of the Moon (the alternate way into Mordor, which Isildur originally built) is unguarded, or at least inhabited only by "dreadful things" (2: 316)—that is, by Shelob. Is Gollum telling the truth here, or is he lying in order to obtain the Ring? Frodo believes that Gollum did leave Mordor by means of his own cunning rather than by the directive of Sauron: "For one thing, he noted that Gollum used *I*, and that seemed usually to be a sign, on its rare appearances, that some remnants of old truth and sincerity were for the moment on top" (2: 318). Gollum's consciousness has been enhanced to the point that his sense of self ("I") has begun to return—that which distinguishes him from mere being (*Gollum*) and therefore marks him as capable of moral choice. Indeed, Gollum now speaks in complete sentences rather than baby talk, and his conversation reflects rational patterns of thought.

Good service, in the next few sections of book 4, proves to be more complex and knotty than the good master anticipates. The rabbits that Gollum catches and Sam cooks give them away by their smoke—but Sam the Good Servant betrays them to Faramir, Good Steward of Gondor and a helpful friend who then, Gandalf-like, rescues and revives them with food, water, and, best of all, sleep. Good service leads to better service. Furthermore, although Sam inadvertently reveals the presence of the Ring to Faramir (2: 366), his failure (or treachery) might have led to Faramir's seizure of the Ring (a matching treachery) but does not. Finally, Faramir, good Steward that he is, wishes to shoot Gollum, because he has seen (and fished in) the Forbidden Pool, but is prevented by Frodo, who then himself "betrays" Gollum's trust in him by summoning him in order to have Faramir bind him for his own protection: "His heart sank. This was too much like trickery. He did not really fear that Faramir would allow Gollum to be killed, but he would probably make him prisoner and bind him; and certainly what Frodo did would seem a treachery to the poor treacherous creature. It would probably be impossible ever to make him understand or believe that Frodo had saved his life in the only way he could. What else could he do?—to keep faith, as near as might be, with both sides" (2: 376–77).

Faramir correctly advises Frodo not to trust Gollum (2: 381), and yet Frodo has promised to protect him and to follow him to Mordor. To violate that pact would be treachery on Frodo's part: "The servant has a claim on the master for service, even service in fear" (2: 375). All of them (except Faramir) in these chapters seem to fail through treachery, but it is apparent treachery only. Even Sam's unthinking desire to cook the rabbits—the providing of physical sustenance to enable clear or moral choices—reflects a strong motivation to serve his master. This it accomplishes better than he might have hoped, because of the resultant rest and refreshment they obtain through Faramir's discovery of them. Even the unwitting revelation of the Ring's presence tests Faramir's service; he succeeds where his brother Boromir has failed. The smoke is a signal, a communication to others, in a land without language. To cook one's food is a sign also of civilization (no raw fish for these hobbits). And to resist the desire for the Ring proves the excellence of one's Stewardship—proves indeed one's humility and lack of selfishness.

The respite in the Garden of Gondor thus opens a "Window in the West" for each of these good servants to see more clearly, to understand (each other and oneself) better, and accordingly to hope more firmly in the future. Given the greatest barrier to their mission—despair, an internal failure of understanding, or the death of the Self, *Mordor*—the apparent signs of failure here are actually signs of survival, continuation, and life. They *do* eat; Gollum *does* come when summoned; Faramir does *not* kill Gollum, imprison Frodo, or seize the Ring. Sam therefore *does* serve the mission better than he imagines. And the insight into themselves and into their own resilience and dependability strengthens their hope. The episode thus functions analogously to the *palantír* episode at the end of book 3: if the *palantír* allows the gazer to see far, the "Window in the West" allows the gazer to see *close*, to gaze inward. The episode also functions analogously to the Lothlórien episode in book 2, when Galadriel offers Frodo and Sam the opportunity to look into her mirror and foresee the future in order to arm themselves with the weapon of knowledge (as Gandalf's history of the Ring has armed Frodo with knowledge of the past in book 1).

The City of the Ringwraiths, or the Tower of the Moon, differs from Isengard and the Tower of Orthanc in the emptiness of its intelligence (Orthanc signifies "Cunning Mind"—perverse and perverted intelligence): "In the walls and tower windows showed, like countless black holes looking inward into emptiness; but the topmost course of the tower revolved slowly, first one way and then another, a huge ghostly head leering into the night" (2: 397). The wall and tower of Minas Morgul ("Tower of Black-Magic") were originally named Minas Ithil ("Tower of the Moon") before capture and inhabitation by the Nazgûl. In this tower close to Cirith Ungol,

"Pass of the Spider," Frodo's loyalty to his best self and to the mission is tested by his desire to put on the Ring and thus reveal his presence in Mordor to Sauron. The spiritual and intellectual emptiness of Minas Morgul attests to the blankness and indifference to any choice at all as the chief peril to Frodo's success now.

Accordingly, when Frodo desires to put on the Ring as the Black Rider pauses before their hiding place (2: 400-1), he initially dissociates himself from the will, moving his hand toward the Ring: "It took his hand, and as Frodo watched with his mind, not willing it but in suspense (as if he looked on some old story far away), it moved the hand inch by inch towards the chain upon his neck. Then his own will stirred; slowly it forced the hand back and set it to find another thing, a thing lying hidden near his breast" (2: 401). The phial of Galadriel counters the nihilism and domination that threaten him, at least here. The phial also helps him turn away Shelob when the hobbits reach the top of the stairs and the tunnel guarded by the malicious spider (2: 419). (Frodo continues to feel, however, that Shelob's eyes "are looking at me, or thinking about me: making some other plan, perhaps" [2: 421].) And the elven blade Sting cuts through the net of cobwebs halting their progress through the dark tunnel. But neither is sufficient against the malice of Shelob and the treachery of Gollum: Shelob captures Frodo and Gollum lunges at Sam.

These twin adversaries at first glance seem oddly disparate. Gollum has so progressed in moral metamorphosis that his relationship with his master might be characterized as loving and the sameness of the two identified as hobbit: "Then he came back, and slowly putting out a trembling hand, very cautiously he touched [sleeping] Frodo's knee—but almost the touch was a caress. For a fleeting moment, could one of the sleepers have seen him, they would have thought that they beheld an old weary hobbit, shrunken by the years that had carried him far beyond his time, beyond friends and kin, and the fields and streams of youth, an old starved pitiable thing" (2: 411).

Perhaps Tolkien manifests the civilization and humanization (hobbitization?) of Gollum in order to make more horrible Gollum's final treachery in this volume—to allow to be killed what he most loves next to the Precious. Indeed, when Sam surprises him "pawing at master," Gollum is portrayed as "almost spider-like

. . . crouched back on his bent limbs, with his protruding eyes"
(2: 411). Surely he resents Sam's label of "sneak"—that is, he
resists Sam's intolerance of difference in hobbit nature. And yet
what is spiderlike in Gollum is that unthinking and inarticulate
existence which depends for its survival on eating—*gollum.* As Shelob is described, "But still she was there, who was there before
Sauron, and before the first stone of Barad-dûr; and she served
none but herself, drinking the blood of Elves and Men, bloated and
grown fat with endless brooding on her feasts, weaving webs of
shadow; for all living things were her food, and her vomit darkness"
(2: 422). The sheer continuation of nature depends on ingestation
and reproduction of kind but cares nothing for incest or slaughter
of kin—it is mindless and immoral: "Far and wide her lesser
broods, bastards of the miserable mates, her own offspring, that
she slew, spread from glen to glen" (2: 422). She is the *gollum*
counter to Sméagol, "and in past days he had bowed and wor-
shipped her, and the darkness of her evil will walked through all
the ways of his weariness beside him, cutting him off from light and
from regret" (2: 423).

As the principle of unthinking life indifferent to moral choice,
Shelob incarnates the instinct to survive that separates the dead
from the existent. Morally and spiritually, however, the malice she
represents is also indifferent to all else except sentient Self: "Little
she knew of or cared for towers, or rings, or anything devised by
mind or hand, who only desired death for all others, mind and
body, and for herself a glut of life, alone, swollen till the mountains
could no longer hold her up and the darkness could not contain
her" (2: 423). Her desire, then, is for "sweeter meat"—an unabated
hunger, as if she were appetite itself (or Sauron's "cat" [2: 424]). For
this reason she is *more* dangerous even than Gollum: no one can
use logic to analyze her twisted motivations, as Gandalf does with
Saruman, because she is moved solely by appetite in her actions.
Tolkien's point is that food, not treasure, exerts a far more primordial and necessary attraction.

The adversaries of Frodo at the end are many—the will of the
Ring (or of Sauron), operating through himself and on Gollum;
Sauron himself and his Nazgûl; and the mindlessness of Shelob,
his "cat." What may be less clear (because apparently less important and less clearly defined) are how those same adversaries

confront Sam differently and the reasons for his consequent choices in the similarly entitled chapter 10, "The Choices of Master Samwise."

When Sam becomes Ringbearer, he has had little or no opportunity to exercise mastery of self or self-discipline, a handicap underscored by his own difference from Frodo. His genealogy and family history differ from his master's; he is not Baggins-Took, or an orphan, or the nephew of Bilbo. Furthermore, his vocation and class depend more on manual labor and earth-tilling than on the leisurely pursuit of scholarship and books, as was the case with Frodo and Bilbo.

Thus Ringbearer Sam's uncontrolled anger at Gollum initially urges pursuit of the creature in mirror image of the ancient malice of Shelob: "For the moment he had forgotten everything else but the red fury in his brain and the desire to kill Gollum" (2: 427). Later a similar mirroring wrath fuels his attack on Shelob: "No onslaught more fierce was ever seen in the savage world of beasts, where some desperate small creature armed with little teeth, alone will spring upon a tower of horn and hide that stands above its fallen mate" (2: 428). The Phial of Galadriel with its light burns Shelob back into her lair. Most important, it is his hearing rather than his vision that is heightened by wearing the Ring after he has determined Frodo is dead, which means that he can understand the orcs he overhears. This precipitous act of Ring wearing thus affords him the miraculous opportunity to learn that Frodo is *not* dead (2: 444) and to change his disastrous course of action from dutiful Ringbearing to the more appropriate, serviceable rescue of his master. Like Frodo, Galadriel, Gandalf, and Faramir, Sam resists the temptation to become Lord of the Ring: he remains what he is, a servant rather than a master. Indeed, his propitious leaving of Frodo for dead convinces the orcs that this "regular elvish trick" is intended to deter them from capture of the "big fellow with the sharp sword" (2: 443).

Through his new linguistic understanding, Sam determines that Frodo lives—for Shelob never binds with cord unless she's hungry, but she "doesn't eat dead meat" (2: 444). Sam's lesson here and the lesson in this second volume is not only that knowledge, conveyed through language, is power, but that the source of that knowledge is equally important: "You fool," Sam says to himself, as the Gollum-like adversary he last confronts, "he isn't dead and your heart knew it. Don't trust your head, Samwise, it is not the best part of you. The trouble with you is that you never really had any hope" (2: 444). Like Saruman, he has denied hope to himself as well as to Gollum. Like Shelob, he has reacted angrily rather than wisely to this crisis. And like Gollum, he has seemingly abandoned and betrayed his master to dark powers: "Never leave your master, never, never: That was my right rule. And I knew it in my heart. May I be forgiven!" (2: 445).

Saruman, Shelob, Gollum, and Sam—unlikely adversaries but all similar in one way or another. From the great knowledge of Saruman to the inarticulation of Shelob is not so great a step—even Saruman is reduced to inarticulate rage when his schemes are foiled. The anger of all leads to murder, Mordor, and the one tower is keyed to the second, at the edge of the wasteland. At the moment Sam is poised to step over that line, his heart and the fullness of its knowledge rescue him. Through recovery of himself he is able to rescue Frodo and thus facilitate the salvation of Middle-earth.

8

Power and the Community:
The Return of the King

WAR AND THE COMPANY

In *The Two Towers* the splitting of the narrative into two
strands—Frodo and Sam journeying to Mount Doom and the
remainder of the surviving company regrouping—led to further
subdivision, at the end, of, first, Frodo at the Pass and Sam journeying alone and, second, Merry joining Théoden and Pippin and
Gandalf striking out for Gondor. This decimation of both company
and narrative is knitted up in *The Return of the King*, the "Book of
Returns." Aragorn, Legolas, and Gimli ride together to summon the
Dead in chapter 2 while Théoden, Merry, and the Riders of Rohan
head for Minas Tirith. Eventually all three strands will meet in
Minas Tirith, after Frodo and Sam have returned the Ring to its ori-
gins, in book 6.

Thus book 5 may be said to be divided into two parts: in the
first the two parts of the reduced Fellowship must jointly reach
Gondor (chapters 1–6). Once the external battle is fought and con-
cluded, the internal battle(s) of Gondor must be completed
(chapters 7–9)—that is, those battles involving the principal leaders
of both Minas Tirith and the reduced Fellowship. Finally, all the
army of the West proceeds to the Black Gate of Morannon in chapter 10, "The Black Gate Opens," which concludes with the final verbal and physical battle and the final rescue.

The journey to Minas Tirith and then to Cirith Gorgor echoes the journeys to the two towers in the preceding two books (books 3 and 4) and will anticipate the journey of Frodo and Sam to Mount Doom and of all the company *back* to the Shire in book 6. In the cases of both books 5 and 6, the destination appears to be a wasted city (Minas Tirith) or a source of power (Mount Doom). The return to the Shire at the end reminds us that corruption occurs even in the most familiar and nonthreatening community, just as it can affect the most dignified and caring of leaders.

To understand how Tolkien structures his journeys in book 5, then, is to understand his symbolic quest. This quest concerns both the nature of real leadership and power and also the complementary but related theme of language as a reflection of real knowledge and understanding. These qualities are necessary in a true leader and underlie real power, wherever it is found.

The first two strands, those in book 5, play variations on the thematic significance of Pippin's Oath of Service to Denethor in chapter 1. Because this Oath of Service solidifies the relationship between an individual and the community (as represented by a lord or ruler), in this fifth book (one of two books constituting *Return*) its appearance allows Tolkien to zero in on power within a larger construct. The contract to serve the good of the whole also expresses the commitment of the ruler. What the appropriate roles of ruled and ruler might be, in Tolkien's utopian vision, metamorphoses in book 6 in the final "returns" of various kings to their various communities—their "homecoming."

THE RETURN OF THE RULER IN BOOK 5

The miniquest of the fragmented Fellowship in book 5 seeks as its destination not Mordor ("murder," "separation") but Gondor ("Stone-land," in Sindarin). This kingdom of Men was founded by Elendil and ruled by Isildur and Anárion—until the line died out, when it was ruled by the Stewards. The last of these Stewards is Denethor, to be replaced by the true king, Aragorn (or Elessar), in 3019 (e.g., by the end of the trilogy).

The "company" of Pippin and Gandalf seeks Gondor in order to help them resist the Dark Enemy, whose constant attacks have debilitated both the kingdom and the strength of its Steward. The goal, one might say, is not just the community of Gondor but community itself. Gondor is also the destination of the second fragment of the original company, consisting of Aragorn, Gimli, and Merry and joined by Théoden and Faramir (son of Denethor); however, they proceed there not directly but via the Paths of the Dead, to gather the company of the Oathbreakers (3: 64–65). And Éowyn, disguised as Dernhelm, will join them riding with Merry on a single horse.

The Siege at Gondor is followed by the grand battle. The goal of the split-and-then-reunited mini-Fellowship and the Free Peoples is ultimately the Great Battle at the Black Gate to Mordor, on the rampart of Cirith Gorgor, beyond the wasted Tower of the Moon, Minas Morgul, through the wasted land that the Lords of Gondor will reclaim (3: 197). But the grand battle is preceded by a confrontation between the Mouth of Sauron (Lieutenant of the Tower of Barad-dûr, a man and not a Ringwraith) and Gandalf as Protector of the Free World. The Towers of the Teeth at this "Haunted Pass" imply a mouth, a great opening into the heart of Mordor, which the Lieutenant—as the Mouth of Sauron—also accentuates in his verbal antagonism toward the Free Peoples. There is more than one way to fight, however—more than one way into Mordor and more than one way of winning, as Frodo, Sam, and Gollum (as well as the Eagles who rescue the hobbits and the Free Peoples) will prove.

Minas Tirith (Tower of Guard), the major city of man, reflects in its iconography the nature of Gondor as "stone land," a place of blight and paralysis. It is in fact a city of gates that foreshadows the Black Gate at the end of book 5. The Great Gate of Minas Tirith, to anticipate the Black Gate at Morannon at the book's end, focuses the reader's attention on the image of ingress and egress as dominant throughout this third volume celebrating the *Return* of the King (my emphasis). It boasts seven levels, each built into the hill, each with a wall, gate, and four directions: "The gates were not set in a line: the Great Gate in the City Wall was at the east point of the circuit, but the next faced half south, and the third half north, and so to and fro upwards; so that the paved way that climbed towards the Citadel turned first this way and then that across the face of the hill. And each time that it passed the line of the Great Gate it went through an arched tunnel, piercing a vast pier of rock whose huge out-thrust bulk divided in two all the circles of the City save the first" (3: 25). In its bifold division of circles, the city reflects the divided community of Men, whose Steward Denethor has arrogated the power of the Ruler to himself.

It is, then, the *passage* of individuals into and out of the community, the whole, and the power they convey within that whole that interests Tolkien. Similarly, it is the communication between two individuals, two leaders, and even two parts of the same body (community, nation, etc.) and their harmonious concord that provides the opportunity for community to exist.

At the top of the pier of rock (an image anticipating Mount Doom?) lies the Citadel, housing the High Court and the Place of the Fountain at the foot of the White Tower, the bastion of the Stewards. This impregnable fortress is protected from all enemies save the Steward and the withering effect of the stone city without its White Trees. The "stone city" *is* stony—a wasted and blighted community linked in its emptiness, its deadly stone, and its lack of human vitality with the Black Land: "Yet it was in truth falling year by year into decay; and already it lacked half the men that could have dwelt at ease there" (3: 26). The White Tree has died: "the falling drops dripped sadly from its barren and broken branches back into the clear water" (3: 27). The White Tree is the sign of its true king, withered now like the line from which Aragorn has sprung.

Denethor, the blighting Steward, is described by Gandalf as a "proud and subtle" father who loved his son Boromir too much (3: 27). Loving one son more than another—the impulsive Boromir rather than the steadfast Faramir—marks an imbalance of passion and a skewed judgment. This characteristic in a ruler (or a Steward) should alert the ruled that a political dysfunction exists. In Denethor its appearance foreshadows the grief and later madness that lead to his demise. Early in book 5 Denethor openly demonstrates his excessive grief over the loss of Boromir and his irrational anger toward the halflings, whose cause led his son to his death, and toward the other son, who should have gone instead of Boromir but did not (3: 29). "Be not unjust in your grief!" Gandalf warns him, but justice is beyond Denethor's reach. So too are tolerance, respect, and praise for accomplishments. When Pippin offers to repay the loss of his son by means of his own service,

Denethor accepts coldly, insisting on the swearing of the legal (feudal) oath of fealty and service to Gondor and to its Lord and Servant (3: 31). Indeed, his first response to the hobbit Pippin when he learns Pippin was there at the time of his son's death is "And how did you escape, and yet he did not, so mighty a man as he was, and only orcs to withstand him?" (3: 30). Denethor's mistake here is both personal and political: his literalism makes him assume that "small" means helpless and weak and that "large" means strong and able. Literalism as a perceptual flaw has troubled Saruman and Sauron. Seeing clearly involves understanding the powerful nature of largess of spirit and goodness of heart, whatever the size and importance of the individual.

The halfling Pippin responds proudly to the scornful suspicion of the old man, in reflection of these flaws: "Little service, no doubt, will so great a lord of Men think to find in a hobbit, a halfling from the northern Shire; yet such as it is, I will offer it, in payment of my debt" (3: 30). Pippin offers his service generously and whitewashes the greedy perfidy of Boromir that led to the breaking of the Fellowship by revealing only the man's sacrificial penance for his misdeed—his attempt to save Merry and Pippin when they were assaulted by orcs.

At issue in this "contest" between the Steward and the would-be servant is the concept of service and obedience. Although Pippin swears an oath to obey, after he is released from the Steward's service later in the narrative he continues to serve—a "disobedience" that actually saves his "nation." His literal infraction of the release actually marks his obedience to the higher goal, of "fealty and service to Gondor," not just to the "Lord and Steward of the realm" (3: 31). At the time he "disobeys," the Steward has become quite mad. Is disobedience of such a ruler disservice?

Elsewhere in this volume Tolkien indicates that it is not—Éowyn, as "Dernhelm," disobeys Théoden's command to stay behind in Rohan but in her disguise as warrior saves Gondor by stabbing the Nazgûl. Later, in book 6, Sam will disobey Frodo's command to take the Ring to Mount Doom after he believes his master is dead, and thus saves Frodo (and Middle-earth). And of course Gollum disobeys his master Frodo when he bites off his ring finger in an ambiguous act one may interpret as either service or disservice—to Frodo, the Precious, or Middle-earth. Always in

Tolkien the lesser is greater, just as the Steward who serves is the true Ruler—and just as he whose arrogance insists on absolute fealty from servants or whose aspirations lead to tyranny is the inept king.

Denethor's verbal contest with Gandalf after Pippin's offer of service (3: 31–33) reminds the reader of Wormtongue's similar contest at the Hall of Rohan and of Saruman's at Isengard. Here the problem of conflict arises not so much from the unmasking of the unfaithful servant (Wormtongue) or of the guileful and cunning wizard (Saruman) as from the misguided and destructive "Service" offered by a self-deceived "Steward." When Denethor first commands Pippin to relate the last adventures of Boromir, Gandalf chides him with what seems to be self-indulgence, given the great battle fought by Théoden and the fall of Saruman that should occupy the thoughts of Gondor's Steward (3: 31). Denethor puts his own grief, and his own self, ahead of Gondor's troubles because "I know already sufficient of these deeds for my own counsel against the menace of East" (3: 32)—largely as a result of the hidden *palantír* he uses. This power to see betrays him and compels him to lie and deceive others, "for though the stones be lost," Denethor claims, "still the lords of Gondor have keener sight than lesser men, and many messages come to them" (3: 32). The Stone that he imagines serves him has blinded him to the need for counsel, communication, and help from others like Gandalf.

Denethor's grief and mental imbalance (probably caused by gazing into the Stone and thus locking wills with the indomitable Eye of Sauron, which no man may best) work themselves into the session with Pippin by means of checked "rising wrath and impatience" (3: 32). And when Gandalf chastises Denethor for making the wizard sit by while he discourses with the hobbit, Denethor's suspicion and paranoia burst forth: "Yet the Lord of Gondor is not to be made the fool of other men's purposes, however worthy" (3: 33). He regards the rule of Gondor as "mine, and no other man's, unless the king should come again" (3: 33). But of course Gandalf corrects his perception of Gandalf as self-serving, for the wizard rules no realm and cares only for "all worthy things that are in peril as the world now stands" (3: 33), "for I also am a steward" (3: 33).

Foils for Denethor, Gandalf and Pippin have also concealed a secret—that Aragorn the king is returning and that he and not Boromir guided the company out of Moria. This secret must be shielded from the hidden ambition of the Steward, whose service to the idea of the King of Gondor will be severely tested by this return.

The pride of Denethor arises from a distorted vision, a selfishness that may be akin to lack of self-love and respect, and a mental imbalance and wrong judgment that disregard the Other. Yet as father of both Boromir and Faramir, he contains both evil and good. While "the blood of Westernesse runs nearly true in him" (3: 35), courtesy, love, and generosity are all qualities missing in this man-who-would-be-king.

The courtesy and generosity of the servant Peregrin (no longer called merely Pippin) stand in stark contrast to the ruler's cold arrogance. Appropriately, his new friend Beregond, father of the young Bergil (3: 48), who has been assigned to teach him the passwords, offers him companionship and ultimately service at the most desperate of times. Even the youthful lad Bergil fears being sent away with the women—marginalized once again—and yet, like so many of the unlikely heroes of *Rings*, courageously serves his "master" and his country in ways unanticipated by even his father, Beregond.

Merry's loving and spontaneous commitment of his service to Théoden in chapter 2 is the inverse image of Pippin's legal obligation to "repay" Denethor for the untimely loss of his son. The two acts share an emphasis on the unimportance of the hobbit servants: "Don't leave me behind," cries Merry. "I don't want to be laid aside, like baggage to be called for when all is over" (3: 53). Merry's service to Théoden will indeed save him, just as Pippin's "disservice" to Denethor saves Gondor. The difference stems from the difference in oath: Merry lovingly swears fealty to the man rather than obligingly to the nation: "Filled suddenly with love for this old man, he knelt on one knee, and took his hand and kissed it. 'May I lay the sword of Meriadoc of the Shire on your lap, Théoden King?' he cried. 'Receive my service, if you will'" (3: 59). And Théoden anoints him as "Meriadoc, esquire of Rohan," rather than mere servant of Gondor, the new role granted to Pippin.

Aragorn's summoning of the Dead synthesizes the twin hobbit significations of service. The Oathbreakers serve Aragorn now because they failed to serve his ancestor Isildur, which resulted in the loss of the kingship. The King of the Mountains had sworn allegiance to him, but when Isildur came to fight Sauron, because the Men of the Mountains worshiped Sauron, they refused. The Sleepless Dead will admit no living human through their Gates except the returning King, who will grant them eternal rest after fulfillment of their past obligation. Their past disservice (unlike Pippin's future "disservice") has caused disaster; it is ameliorated by their present and future service, which will help (like Merry's loving service to Théoden) save Middle-earth.

The leadership styles of Denethor and Théoden (whose names are mirror images of each other: Den-ethor and Théo-den) are equally complementary. The tyrant commands his followers by edict, rule, law; the true leader commands through respect and love, like a benign father to a son. Merry thus appropriately cries, "As a father you shall be to me" (3: 59), while Pippin, like the ignored and unloved son Faramir, suffers from the selfish preferring of Denethor for his lost dead son.

The resurrection of the past—the memory of the disservice of the Men of the Mountain that leads to their summoning—helps to heal old wounds dividing Man and Man (read: brother and brother). The terror evoked by the company's passing through the Dead Marshes is mastered by the decimated company of man, elf, and dwarf. Such courage contrasts with what, on Denethor's part, must be termed cowardice and inability to master his own grief and despair. His losing his head and his subsequent irrationality signify the madness that leads to his self-destruction, his suicide on the pyre of Boromir. Unlike the Men of the Mountain, this man of Minas Tirith succumbs to the past, to death, to despair. By so doing he also fails in his role as Steward to the King.

If Denethor's will is no match for Sauron's in the battle of the *palantír*, Aragorn's is just barely a match. The rightful owner of this visionary stone manifests himself to Sauron (himself a Bad Steward). In this "Return" of the King lie further demoralization and growing despair of the darkest of lords. At the same time this contest gives Aragorn insight into an unexpected peril awaiting Minas Tirith: the city will be lost in 10 days unless he travels via the Paths of the Dead to summon the Oathbreakers (3: 64–65).

The summoning of Théoden and Rohan to help at the Siege of Gondor (chapter 3) does result in the leaving behind of two who would serve, Merry and Éowyn, the latter of whom Aragorn in chapter 2 insisted must stay behind. Both Merry and Éowyn disobey their beloved lords—Merry riding along undercover with Éowyn, and Éowyn disguised as Dernhelm. At the Battle of the Pelennor Fields (chapter 6) both will redeem their disobedience, the shield-maiden Éowyn by circumventing the prophecy that "No living man may hinder me" (3: 141) and killing the Nazgûl Lord. Merry's service to Théoden—to stay with the felled King—rests on the courage of his oath as King's man and as "son" (3: 141) and to Éowyn-Dernhelm—to protect her both from the Ringwraith and from *herself* (3: 140): "For into Merry's mind flashed the memory of the face that he saw at the riding from Dunharrow: the face of one that goes seeking death, having no hope. Pity filled his heart and great wonder, and suddenly the slow-kindled courage of his race awoke. . . . She should not die, so fair, so desperate!" (3: 142). The despair he fights is *her* despair, as Pippin must fight Denethor's, and Aragorn, the despair of Men in the face of Sauron's power reflected in the past treachery of the Men of the Mountain.

If we recall that the Great Gate of Minas Tirith allows both ingress and egress, the passing outward and the returning inward, and that return is the major goal of this last volume in the trilogy, it is important to note that Pippin is the gatekeeper at the moment. Pippin's service to Denethor begins as menial and domestic. Replacing the esquire of Denethor's chamber, he must wait on the Steward, performing his errands and even singing to him (3: 96). A prince masquerading as a clown and a servant ("the Prince of the Halflings, that folk [elves] had called him" [3: 97]), Pippin sinks into a gloom that threatens to undermine his necessary role. The opposite to Denethor's self-aggrandizing behavior as Steward, this humble masquerade in effect has been Aragorn's role for years as the Ranger Strider. The regal character of both man and halfling emerges best in the courage and rational balance necessary to any true leader in combating demoralization.

Nevertheless, the "poisonous despair" that strikes their hearts most keenly is that of the Black Riders—a despair akin to death of the spirit (3: 99). Faramir, like Aragorn and Pippin, is also capable of withstanding demoralization and despair: "When he saw the pale face of Faramir he caught his breath. It was the face of one who has been assailed by a great fear or anguish, but has mastered it and now is quiet. . . . Here was one with an air of high nobility such as Aragorn at times revealed . . . one of the Kings of Men born into a later time, but touched with the wisdom and sadness of the Elder Race. . . . He was a captain that men would follow, that he would follow, even under the shadow of the black wings" (3: 101).

The meeting of Faramir and his father, Denethor (chapter 4, "The Siege of Gondor"), clearly and strikingly shows the reader Tolkien's definition of the capable versus the flawed ruler. The truths revealed in this meeting portray a father suspicious of his son's fidelity, judgment, and love, a Steward greedy to rule not only Gondor but all of Middle-earth, and a son whose courage resists the Power of the Ring, unlike his brother Boromir (whose failure Gandalf finally reveals to the old man). Denethor accuses Faramir of listening more to Gandalf's counsel than to his (3: 103), a mistake in love, so he believes, but not Tolkien. To make one's duty to one's father supersede one's duty to one's nation is treachery. But Denethor accuses his son of greater crimes: of living rather than dying in place of his beloved son Boromir:

> "Do you wish then," said Faramir, "that our places had been exchanged?"
>
> "Yes, I wish that indeed," said Denethor. "For Boromir was loyal to me and no wizard's pupil. He would have remembered his father's need, and would not have squandered what fortune gave. He would have brought me a mighty gift." (3: 104)

But the Ring is no gift to be given to an imperious father by a dutiful son. Denethor confuses love with service, desire with need, power with value. Perhaps Denethor's greatest crime is to put himself before all of Middle-earth: to imagine the "mighty gift" of the Ring as a test of his son's love.

Faramir nearly succumbs to his father's bitterness and despair, but his love for this mad old man permits him to be tolerant, self-controlled, and understanding. "For a moment Faramir's restraint gave way" (3: 104), Tolkien notes, for Denethor himself had commanded Boromir to go, while Faramir stayed in Ithilien. The ruling Steward sends his favorite son on a mission that he foresees will enable him to have true power, through the Ring. Ironically the other son stays behind as a Steward who serves—ideally fulfilling the more humble role of the Steward. And yet in Tolkien's schema the true king *is* a Steward, or servant, of his people. According to this definition, Faramir from the beginning should have been recognized as the more loyal and trustworthy of leaders.

The Ring offers the truest litmus for kingship, and even so it prevails over the strongest of wills. As Gandalf warns Denethor, who imagines Boromir would have brought the Ring back to him, "Yet you deceive yourself. He would have stretched out his hand to this thing, and taking it he would have fallen. He would have kept it for his own" (3: 104). The beauty and power of the Ring would, of course, also have prevailed over the disordered brain of Denethor, whose advice is to have kept it "hidden dark and deep" (3: 105), presumably in the Citadel at Gondor. Most likely, as Gandalf suspects, Denethor would have been tempted to use it because he is weak: "Nonetheless, I do not trust you" (3: 105), the wizard admits. The threat is that it will "burn your mind away." What Gandalf does not know is that Denethor has already been burned, by secretly using the Stone and revealing himself to Sauron's Eye.

How is the man Denethor different from the wizard Saruman, who also used the Stone and who also wanted the Ring for his own? Saruman's cold rationality grew out of pride, but it never deteriorated into madness. In contrast, Denethor's intelligence, spurred by pride and desire, degenerates into madness out of grief over his son's loss. It is a perversion of excess love, or wrongly directed love, that motivates the Steward of Gondor. His preference for one son over the other reveals a deeper flaw: a self-seeking and King Lear–like "love" within the family that mirrors his self-aggrandizing role with the community of Gondor. Saruman, in short, has no sons, and while he is charged with the role of Steward of the White Council, he seems to care little for the community and rules his fiefdom as a tyrant. Denethor initially does serve as a Steward and also degenerates into tyranny, but he has no special distinction, talent, or faculty (like wizardry) beyond his external badge. As such he is a more likely foil for the hobbit Sam, servant of Frodo. Denethor and Sam epitomize service within two communities, human and hobbit. It is the "witless halfling" and not the crafty man who demonstrates greater service to his lord, the lord of Gondor, and all of Middle-earth.

The contest within Denethor occurs between his desire for the Ring (read: kingship) and his love for his son Faramir (read: father-hood). Most horribly, Denethor sends away his remaining son to what seems certain death as a final test of Faramir's service, to defend the River and the Pelennor (3: 109). Faramir asks of him, "If I should return, think better of me," but even Denethor's response is conditional: "That depends on the manner of your return" (3: 109).

The return of the hero (an event important in the classical epic) is used as a unifying image in *Return*. Boromir has returned as a dead hero to Gondor (or so his father believes); Faramir will return as a live hero and Steward. Aragorn, in the sixth and last book, does return alive also, but as King rather than Steward. In another sense the Ring and the "Lord of the Rings" (Frodo? or Gollum? or Sam?) return to Mordor and Mount Doom. If Gollum never again departs, remaining Lord of the Rings in Mordor, then Frodo and Sam both return to the Shire, Frodo as hero and Sam as servant to the hero. Yet it is Sam who becomes Mayor of the Shire, while Frodo departs for the Grey Havens. Heroism for Tolkien seems to debilitate his heroes. Service, in contrast, strengthens them to take on political roles within the community—allows them, in short, to survive. Without servants *and* heroes, Tolkien argues, the commu-nity remains imbalanced.

At the end of book 5, Denethor loses his internal battle with his own madness, revealing that the greater enemy is nearly always internal rather than external. Indeed, as we have seen earlier, dread and despair constitute the primary weapons of Sauron, along with exploitation of others to work his own will. As Denethor pro-claims, "He uses others as his weapons. So do all great lords, if they are wise, Master Halfling. Or why should I sit here in my tower and think, and watch, and wait, spending even my sons?" (3: 111). The awful image of sons as money to spend reveals the near-total moral degeneration of Denethor. But his last vestige of humanity is his love for his sons, and Sauron will push that to the limit to drive Denethor over the edge, from despair to total madness and suicide.

Faramir does return, seemingly dead, after heroic deeds —much like his brother Boromir. But just as Boromir performed those deeds to atone for his catastrophic moment of greed and desire with Frodo, so too did Faramir perform those deeds to prove his love for and service to his father and lord, Denethor. In one case Boromir did fail; in the other Faramir did not in fact fail Denethor at all. Moreover, Boromir remains dead, whereas Faramir is returned to life by Aragorn, the healing king.

The main difference between the return of Boromir and that of Faramir, however, resides in the effect of the return on their father and lord. Denethor's face is described as "more deathlike than his son's" (3: 115), and indeed this final blow pushes him into the ultimate despair or hopelessness that kills him. Tolkien underscores what might be termed Denethor's losing his head by means of the enemy's hurling of heads of warriors into the beleaguered and surrounded city. The strategy is to enhance the city's despair—its collective loss of hope and rationality: "For yet another weapon, swifter than hunger, the Lord of the Dark Tower had: dread and despair" (3: 117). In Denethor's case the guilt arising from his angry command to Faramir becomes unbearable. He not only has sent two sons to their deaths (he must argue to himself) but has severed all hope of his own (as well as his nation's) posterity through progeny, for Boromir and Faramir seem to be the sole successors to the stewardship: "I sent my son forth, unthanked, unblessed, out into needless peril, and here he lies with poison in his veins. Nay, nay, whatever may now betide in war, my line too is ending, even the House of the Stewards has failed. Mean folk shall rule the last remnant of the Kings of Man, lurking in the hills until all are hounded out" (3: 118).

The despair of Denethor is grounded in grief, guilt, pain, hopelessness—and lack of imagination. He never imagines or guesses that the King has returned, that the "witless Halfling" will make it to Mount Doom and save the world. Once again literalism (or what might be defined as the reality of "what meets the eye") remains pernicious in its limitations, chiefly the power to destroy, for Denethor's final commands are hopeless, suicidal: he commands the messengers to "Go back and burn," he releases Pippin from his service in order to die, and he enters into the House of Stewards with his dying son Faramir to create a pyre for them both.

It is another "witless Halfling" who disobediently countermands Denethor's final suicidal orders. "Your master is not himself. . . . Do nothing until Gandalf comes!" (3: 122), Pippin cautions the servant. And to Beregond he presents a choice: between obeying his orders to remain at his post and saving Faramir's life by fetching Gandalf (3: 123). Through Pippin's disobedience Tolkien presents the imaginative solution to Denethor's mad literalism and hopelessness: service implies a thinking allegiance to a lord. A mad lord, whatever his orders to others, is not capable of leading his people, caring for the community, or even considering thoughtfully his own welfare. In book 5, as in book 6, the "witless Halfling" ironically saves the community from the abuses of his "superior"—here Pippin; in book 6, Frodo, Sam, and Gollum.

The Lord of the Nazgûl who breaks through the Gate to Gondor (3: 125) confronts, then, three "Lords," all differing types of leadership. Gandalf the wizard verbally refuses him admittance; mad Denethor as the titular lord of Gondor for all purposes gives up his will, after giving up his hope and his son (3: 155), and dies resisting the rescue at hand; and Aragorn proves his kinghood not just by wielding a sword but also by laying on the healing hands of the king ("*and so shall the rightful king be known*" [3: 169]).

The hobbits Merry and Pippin similarly provide foils for the failed steward Denethor in their courageous and dedicated service to Rohan and Gondor: Merry disobeys his master's orders (secretly accompanying Dernhelm to battle), and Pippin obeys his master's command to leave his post but not to leave his service (seeking help from Gandalf for the wounded Faramir and the leaderless city). In a sense each demonstrates a signal skill of the ideal ruler who serves the people. Merry performs valorously in battle as he attempts to save Dernhelm, and Pippin attempts to help console the grieving and mad Denethor, to save the life of Faramir, and to heal his companion Merry, wounded in battle. The servant serves by means of his courage and martial prowess and also by means of his care, nurturing, and healing knowledge. What has traditionally been regarded as gender-linked behavior is here gender-neutral (note that it is the wisewoman of Gondor, Ioreth, who spells out the definition of the king as healer [3: 169]).

Denethor fails as father and as steward-ruler because he gives in too readily to hopelessness and despair (he fears too easily that Faramir will die and that Gandalf will be the new ruler of Gondor [3: 156–58]). Resisting his powerlessness to control the fate of his son and of his own city, he preserves the one power he believes he does have, to kill himself. Gandalf warns him that "authority is not given to you, Steward of Gondor, to order the hour of your death. . . . And only the heathen kings, under the domination of the Dark Power did thus, slaying themselves in pride and despair, murdering their kin to ease their own death" (3: 157). Denethor's horrible pride is of course nurtured into madness by the *palantír* he uses to engage the Eye of Sauron. He imagines now that Gandalf covets his throne and that the wizard has stolen his son's love (3: 158). Denethor's failure, then, is one marked by warped perception of the truth, disordered imagination, inability to love—indeed, a lack of that self-love which would permit a less jealously guarded filial loyalty—overweening ambition and covetousness, and a will uncontrolled by rational process. "But in this at least thou shalt not defy my will: to rule my own end" (3: 158), Denethor cries at the moment of his fiery self-immolation and the deliberate breaking of his Steward's staff.

The healing power of the king in the Houses of Healing (chapter 8) extends to Éowyn, Faramir, and Merry, who are all sick with the malady of the Black Shadow that comes from the Nazgûl. The malady resembles the illness experienced by Frodo among the barrow-wights and Black Riders; it begins with dream and is followed by silence and deadly cold, then death. The cure is *athelas*, or *kingsfoil*, a herb whose restorative power is compared with the "memory of dewy mornings of unshadowed sun in some land of which the fair world in Spring itself is but a fleeting memory" (3: 173). The rejuvenation it works on the psyche is even more pronouncedly positive: when Faramir awakens, he responds to Aragorn's healing service with words that echo the Gospel: "a light of knowledge and love was kindled in his eyes, and he spoke softly. 'My lord, you called me. I come. What does the king command?'" (3: 173). The power of kingsfoil resides even in its summons to service: it spurs renewed vitality as a response to solicitude and love. The herb images forth the obedient love of servant for master, the protective love of master for servant.

Éowyn and Merry must also be restored: one to her more realistic role as beloved of Faramir rather than of Aragorn; the other to his natural role as hobbit. Éowyn's restoration depends, then, on a psychological bridging of her despair over the loss of Théoden and in a sense of Aragorn, just as Faramir's restoration depended on the bridging of grief over the loss of his father. In each case recuperation transcends merely physical healing. And in each case hope as the remedy for despair arises from love offered by the king.

In Merry's case his hurt is ameliorated in large part by his own "strong and gay" spirit. He is naturally ebullient and has lost not a father but a lord, Théoden. Moreover, he is a hobbit, not a human being like Éowyn and Faramir: "His grief he will not forget; but it will not darken his heart, it will teach him wisdom" (3: 177). The *athelas* that restores him physically is supplemented by that *west-mansweed* which all hobbits love to smoke and which signals the return of his natural hobbit vitality. In short, Merry is not given to despair in the way of his human counterparts.

If Aragorn reveals through his regal skills the antidote to his servants' despair in book 5, Gandalf also reveals through his wizardry a second antidote to communal and collective despair. In a sense as wizard Gandalf guides and protects all of Middle-earth, although he continually rejects the insignia and tools of power (for example, he returns the key of Gondor to Beregond until the true ruler can accept his mission). His counsel to the lords awaiting battle (chapter 9) is as ameliorative and restorative as the *athelas* of Aragorn: he uses his wits to gaze steadfastly at the truth and turn it to their advantage. Because Denethor has revealed the ominous truth (gleaned from the Stone) that "against the Power that has now arisen there is no victory" (3: 189), Gandalf asks them not to despair but to "ponder the truth in these words" (3: 189). Victory must come some other way than through might and physical advantage. Tolkien suggests that a steady gaze at what *is*—present reality—has greater efficacy than the self-deceptive gaze at what *will be*—future reality—in the Stone. This efficacy is reflected in Gandalf's brilliance in using reality to his own advantage: it is true that against Sauron there is no victory, but it is also true that the return of the Ring (read: King) to Mount Doom does not imply a battle and that this return is the most effective means of undermining Sauron. Thus to distract Sauron from that mission and to delay his inevitable discovery, the company *must* assemble for the grand battle. It is what Sauron himself believes they are foolhardy enough to do. And the Eagles (who spot Frodo at Mount Doom) will also "save" the Free Peoples at the last moment—a truly miraculous sign of natural grace and of that Return of power to its original source, healing Nature.

That sign of grace is necessary to combat the near-despair that grips Gandalf at the last moment. The Messenger reveals Sam's short sword, a gray cloak with elven-brooch, and a coat of mithril-mail worn by Frodo (3: 203), perceiving quickly the fear and horror of the company. Gandalf does not know whether Frodo is alive or dead or whether the Ring is safe, but he must use his imagination and wisdom to think like Sauron—to believe that *little* means inferior and that *power* means physical strength. Thus he plumes up sufficient courage to say, "This is much to demand for the delivery of one servant" (3: 205).

Imagination, wisdom, hope, courage—all these qualities are vital in a leader, a king. But they are also vital in a steward and a servant. Pippin overcomes his horror of hearing Gandalf's rejection of the Mouth's terms: "he had mastered himself" (3: 207). This self-mastery allows him to save the wounded Beregond from death at the claws of a troll-chief, despite his own despair ("it seemed best to him to die soon. . . . 'But now I must do my best'" [3: 207]).

All of these qualities reappear in book 6 in two other unlikely heroes, Frodo the scholarly hobbit and Sam the gardener, like the learned wizard and the "witless halfling," only apparently useless and unable. Powerless, small, but endowed with perseverance and pluck, the two (along with the despicable Gollum) complete their mission and save Middle-earth by means of a single unwitnessed act of renunciation. The act does not require physical strength, size, or skills; nor for that matter does it depend particularly on intelligence. It is a moral act par excellence, an act shared in by the "community" of Frodo, Sam, and Gollum (in that each needs the help of the other in order to succeed in the act), and it epitomizes Tolkien's vision of the power of the community to heal and knit up the social fabric.

HOMECOMING IN BOOK 6

The dilemma in book 6 belongs to the individual, whether Sam or Frodo. The narrowed focus of Tolkien's attention thus permits an interiorized drama to play out against the wasted, blasted landscape of Mordor and Mount Doom. Against death and doom, it is true, Tolkien's morality play portrays the individual reclaiming the power of the courageous self to heal and guide itself by means of imagination, hope, courage, and wisdom. We have, however, moved inward—*as if* inside the soul itself, whether that of Frodo or Sam: "But they were far beyond aid, and no thought could yet bring any help to Samwise Hamfast's son; he was *utterly alone*" (3: 212; my italics). The bearing of the Ring invites spiritual contest—a psychomachia (soul debate) in the most narrow sense.

The focus in book 6 initially falls on Sam, then Frodo, then on both in their battle with Gollum at the end. Each "Ringbearer" reacts to the weight of the Ring differently, one with heightened senses, one with heightened knowledge, and one with heightened force. For Sam his sense of hearing is sharpened so that he overhears the orcs Shagrat and Gorbag fighting in the tower and guesses rightly that Frodo is not dead (3: 213). And when he searches the tower futilely for the entrance to Frodo's prison and his light burns out, he counters his own despair with the defiant singing of an original composition: "And then suddenly new strength rose in him, and his voice rang out, while words of his own came unbidden to fit the simple tune" (3: 226). Because of this song, Snaga the guard orc opens his door to quiet the "squeaking" and Sam is able to discover the means of entry—through the rooftop. The second hobbit, Frodo, we have seen earlier in his role as Ringbearer, and when he demands the Ring back from his faithful servant he (once again) imagines Sam as a thieving orc, "a foul little creature with greedy eyes and slobbering mouth" (3: 230). Because his long experience with the Ring has trained him in the oppression of these passing visions, however, he is able to withstand the "clarifying vision" offered by the Ring and to see "blindly"—that is, to see humanly, that "there was Sam kneeling before him, his face wrung with pain, as if he had been stabbed in the heart; tears welled from his eyes" (3: 230).

The Ring for Frodo tricks him into a clear and omniscient vision (like that of the Stone) that is unfortunately only partly true. Indeed, Sam *is* reluctant to give up the Ring, for he asks if he can't share Frodo's job (3: 230), and he *has* taken it from Frodo because he believed his master was dead. But he has successfully weathered the Temptation of the Ring (3: 216), either to forbear the Ring or to claim it and challenge the Power; his earthy, sensuous nature produces visions different from those of his master: "Wild fantasies arose in his mind; and he saw Samwise the Strong, Hero of the Age, striding with a flaming sword across the darkened land, and armies flocking to his call as he marched to the overthrow of Barad-dûr. And then all the clouds rolled away, and the white sun shone, and at his command the vale of Gorgoroth became a garden of flowers and trees and brought forth fruit" (3: 216).

The chief peril for both these Ringbearers is not themselves—that is, their understanding—but their moral and physical strength in the face of the strength and madness of Gollum yearning for his Precious. The third hobbit has been too weakened by his many years of Ringbearing to resist either his heightened physical power as they approach Mount Doom or the frenzies of his disordered imagination. Thus he becomes an appropriate foil for *both* Sam and Frodo together, who act in the final stages of the journey as one. Frodo must bear the Ring, and Sam must (literally) bear the debilitated Frodo as they near the precipice. What enables them to continue are the willpower of Sam and the Eucharistic-like grace of elven waybread, or *lembas*. Whenever Sam seems to sink into despair, some new hope revives him: "But even as hope died in Sam, or seemed to die, it was turned to a new strength. Sam's plain hobbit-face grew stern, almost grim, as the will hardened in him, and he felt through all his limbs a thrill, as if he was turning into some creature of stone and steel that neither despair nor weariness nor endless barren miles could subdue" (3: 259). The second aid, *lembas*, feeds the will and strengthens endurance (3: 262).

The adversary in the Land of Shadow operates by means of great violence and divisiveness. For example, the watchers over Frodo quarrel to the death ("Mordor" indeed) over Frodo's mithril-mail. Furthermore, the Lord of the Ringwraiths has used the Tower of Cirith Ungol in which Frodo was imprisoned not so much to keep out intruders as to keep the inhabitants of Mordor *in* (3: 215). And the sheer weight of the Ring deadens Frodo's progress across the blasted landscape. The madness that will overtake Gollum at the end nearly divides the warring selves of Frodo: "Stand away! Don't touch me!" he warns Sam when the servant offers to bear the Ring for him, and the next moment Frodo confesses sadly, "It is my burden. . . . I could not give it up, and if you tried to take it I should go mad" (3: 263). The split selves of Frodo are matched by two voices in Sam the faithful servant, debating whether he should plan to take up the role of Ringbearer when Frodo weakens to the point of immobility or whether he is able to complete an errand the specific nature of which Frodo has never revealed to him (3: 266). If one voice counsels giving up now because of the impossibility of the mission, the other voice answers with sheer bravado and determination that Sam will continue *even if* he must carry Frodo, even "if it breaks my back and heart" (3: 266).

Their means of fighting these various threats consists first of stripping away all that is extraneous (including the cooking gear) to lighten their mutual load—initially the Ring (3: 264) and very soon Frodo himself (3: 268). Second, the service Sam renders to Frodo is so great that he becomes body to Frodo's soul. He literally controls Frodo's hand that reaches for the Ring to put it on and thus reveal to Sauron their presence (3: 270). Just as important, he becomes parent to Frodo's child, bearing him on his back "with no more difficulty than if he were carrying a hobbit-child pig-a-back in some romp on the lawns or hayfields of the Shire" (3: 268). Just as the true king heals his subjects in a female and nurturing way, so too does the true servant serve his master. Heroism gives way finally before the simplest love a mother can offer her child, which sustains the will as much as defiance and *lembas*.

The third and final Ringbearer, Gollum, is also their main and final adversary, epitomizing all that is darkest in the hobbit soul—lust, rage, terror. Even so, Gollum addresses himself as Sméagol, the name of his better (hobbitlike) self invoked by Master Frodo to reclaim and civilize him (3: 271). And he has given himself over completely to the ruinous vision of the other as thief experienced by Frodo earlier. Thus the grappling of Gollum and Frodo on the path to Mount Doom in a locked embrace even Sam cannot disentangle suggests a symbolic oneness, as if we are witnessing the darkest night of the soul and one side attempting to master the other. Indeed, Sam's vision of the two portrays the "rivals" (for the Ring) as a "creature now wholly ruined and defeated, yet filled with a hideous lust and rage; and before it stood stern, untouchable now by pity, a figure robed in white, but at its breast it held a wheel of fire" (3: 272).

Frodo as Master ably resists his other Self. Amazingly, Sam protects that other Self because of an overwhelming pity that stays his own hand: "But deep in his heart there was something that restrained him: he could not strike this thing lying in the dust, for-lorn, ruinous, utterly wretched" (3: 273). It is the quality of empathy that saves Gollum: "He himself, though only for a little while, had borne the Ring, and now dimly he guessed the agony of Gollum's shrivelled mind and body, enslaved to that Ring, unable to find peace or relief ever in life again" (3: 273). The compassion of Sam (even if irritably expressed) renders him once again as maternal and caring—Gollum *is* like a naughty child, and he speaks to the hobbit using childish language: "Go away! Be off! I don't trust you, not as far as I could kick you; but be off. Or I *shall* hurt you, yes, with nasty cruel steel" (3: 273).

At the very end, then, who is master, who servant, who hero, who adversary? Frodo succumbs to the power of the Ring, as he always knew he would, and puts it on his finger, failing in the deed he has come to perform (3: 274). Gollum, who has succumbed long ago to that power, struggles with Frodo and bites off the ring finger. He chants the name "Precious" like a mantra as he dances on the brink and then inadvertently falls into the depths (3: 276). Does he intend to serve the Master so sacrificially in this last faithful gesture of protecting Precious? Does Frodo actually fail as he seems to? They have averted the gaze of Sauron until the final moment. And the Ring *is* returned to the hellish depths of Mount Doom, just as they intended. Frodo reminds him, "Do you remember Gandalf's words: *Even Gollum may have something yet to do*? But for him, Sam, I could not have destroyed the Ring. The Quest would have been in vain, even at the bitter end. So let us forgive him!" (3: 277) Each of the three Ringbearers plays a role in the quest, most of all Gollum, the least significant hobbit of them all.

After these three chapters we return to the Battle of the Free Peoples and the knitting up (or "return") of the narrative in the final six chapters. The "Returns" are many in kind and quality. With battle averted and Sauron undermined, a springlike mood of natural healing returns to Middle-earth, especially to Ithilien. Sam reveals that he feels "like spring after winter, and sun on the leaves; and like trumpets and harps and all the songs I have ever heard!" (3: 283) The season *is* spring, on the eve of May, in its annual return. The rebirth of Middle-earth is matched by the healing of two "stewards," Éowyn of Rohan and Faramir of Gondor—the one hurt in spirit and the other in body. Amazingly, the proud shield-maiden

Éowyn is healed by the love of the gentle Steward Faramir. Éowyn warns, "Look not to me for healing! I am a shieldmaiden and my hand is ungentle" (3: 294), when Faramir asks her to ease his care (read: heal his unrequited love with her favor). His "service" to this warrior does heal her coldness, described as frost: when Faramir suggests that she and he must wait in the Houses of Healing instead of riding to battle (now that the war is over), "something in her softened, as though a bitter frost were yielding at the first faint presage of Spring. A tear sprang in her eye and fell down her cheek, like a glistening rain-drop" (3: 294). Faramir's persistent love and kind presence eventually move her to give up her hopeless love for Aragorn and her role as warlike shield-maiden. "I will be a healer, and love all things that grow and are now barren" (3: 300).

The return of the King is marked by mercy balanced with justice. Beregond who spilled blood in the Hollows (an act prohibited by law) and who left his post without permission of Lord or Captain should receive death but instead is appointed to the White Company, the Guard of Faramir, to be captain, because he risked so much to save his lord Faramir.

Aragorn also plants the new tree in the Court of the Fountain, signifying his own fruitful betrothal to Arwen, daughter of Elrond and elf to his man. This joining of two peoples symbolizes concord and harmony on earth in mirrored reflection of the concord between Rohan and Gondor established by the marriage of Éowyn and Faramir. The political and social healing that follows on the return of the King restores harmony and order to the ruled individually and to bodies of the ruled, to the communities that make up Middle-earth. Again, however, the power of the King resides in his ability to heal, to knit together, to bring peace and fruitfulness to the community, to return or renew that which has been torn or debilitated.

The company and its individual members must also return to their respective destinations. The return to the Shire is remarkable chiefly for the necessity of the healing "king" to restore it to its former state. A miniature "Mordor" pillaged by "Sharkey" (Saruman) and his "dog" Worm (Gríma), the community has been terrorized by strong tyrants. The inability of this pair to learn from their experiences—their hard-heartedness—is first witnessed by the hobbits, Lady Galadriel, and Gandalf at the foot of the Misty Mountains.

Saruman rejects the help of Gandalf and self-centeredly imagines the Lady has come there just to gloat over his reduced state (3: 323). Berating and abusing Grima remain Saruman's chief sport, especially as his servant lacks the will to leave him. He manifests envy of the hobbits ("you have all you want, food and fine clothes, and the best weed for your pipes" [3: 324]) and avarice toward Merry when he seizes the pouch of tobacco offered to him by the hobbit and declares it a "repayment in token" (3: 324). Within the Shire the effects of this vicious wizard's rule are seen in the spiked gates at the ends of the Bridge, the inhospitable words of the guard, the fright of the passers-by, the insistence on obeying the orders of the "Chief" and his Big Man (Mr. Lotho, the "Dark Lord" of the Shire) and Saruman (Sharkey). In miniature the entire drama of Sauron and his battle with the Free Peoples is replayed—but to what purpose?

For the purpose of witnessing the return of the lost King, whether named as Frodo, Merry, Pippin—or Sam. Bill Ferny and his like have always lurked near the Shire, but they and their tyrannous desires now dominate the community. In contrast to the other hobbits, the returning heroes are larger and "masterful" (3: 344) in their arms. But what they have returned to is a most unnatural (for hobbits) environment, stripped of tobacco, beer, much of its food, and the peaceful ways of the Shirefolk.

Worse, the returning hobbits are threatened with arrest for Gatebreaking and Tearing up of Rules and Trespassing—their valiant efforts to enter designated as disorderly (3: 346). Freedom has been abridged, military troops have been organized, and sameness and homogeneity (mostly what men want) have been imposed to disempower the "little folk." Frodo, acting consistently, *is* different from the other hobbits, who cower, but his difference (from our educated point of view) is valuable, heroic. He laughs at the arrest threatened by the Shirriff-leader, just as Merry makes the Shirriff march at the front of the company while its members laugh and sing, and Frodo also understands that "Chief" Lotho is probably a prisoner of Saruman at Bag End (in fact he's dead). Merry too is now "different"—he blows the horn of Rohan to raise the people of Hobbiton with the Horn-cry of Buckland. The leadership they provide encourages the "comfortable folk" of Hobbiton to revolt against the oppressive tyranny of Sharkey and his cohort Worm. Their defeat of the jeering men who threaten Farmer Cotton (which results in the death of their leader) rids the community of violence; their defeat of Sharkey rids it of tyranny.

Lotho Pimple is revealed as a puppet Dark Lord whose real estate maneuvers early on resulted in final ownership of much of the Shire; he must be tested in the way the Dark Lord was—indirectly. His greed extended to selling the Shire tobacco and food, selling trees, and inviting in men who took over. But it is Sharkey who controls him now, just as Sauron controlled his Mouth. The men who refuse the commands of "little" Merry are cornered, and many, including their leader, are killed by the valorous hobbit Merry and his Shire followers. The names of the participants in the Battle of Bywater, in 1419, are recorded in a roll included in the Red Book, at the top of which appear the names of two "Captains," Meriadoc and Peregrin.

It is Frodo who must help defeat Sharkey ("Old Man" in Orkish [3: 358]), Worm, and dirty Ted Sandyman and dismantle the mill—after he sees that "this is Mordor. . . . Just one of its works" (3: 367). Worst of all are the disorder and destruction for their own sake that Sharkey regards as one ill turn deserving another (3: 368). Most appropriate is his servant Worm's cursed and enraged murder of the fallen wizard. If Frodo understands how to humiliate Sharkey—that is, by pitying him even though he has attempted to stab Frodo—the hobbit hero would not of his own volition kill the wizard ("He is fallen, and his cure is beyond us; but I would still spare him, in the hope that he may find it" [3: 369]). It is the sadistic treachery of Sharkey that makes Worm snap—his accusation that Worm murdered and perhaps ate Lotho, even if at Sharkey's behest, and his physical and verbal abuse, including a kick in the face and his command to "follow."

The easy "Scouring of the Shire" (as if it were merely a sink of dirty dishes, or a filthy house) is followed by the kind of renaissance enjoyed by Ithilien after the fall of Sauron. Lobelia Sackville-Baggins returns Bag End to Frodo after the news of Lotho's death and wills her fortune for the use of homeless hobbits (3: 372). Frodo functions as Deputy Mayor to reduce the number of Shirriffs, and the Captains Merry and Pippin ferret out the remaining ruffians. Sam is charged with the repair and physical restoration of the village, especially the planting of new trees. The rejuvenative spring of 1420 brings "wonderful sunshine and delicious rain . . . but there seemed something more: an air of richness and growth, and a gleam of beauty beyond that of mortal summers that flicker and pass upon this Middle-earth. All the children born or begotten in that year, and there were many, were fair to see and strong, and most of them had a rich golden hair that had before been rare among hobbits" (3: 375). The fruit is abundant; no one becomes sick. The tobacco crop and the beer are the finest ever. Sam Gamgee marries Rose Cotton (in echo of the weddings of Aragorn and Arwen, Faramir and Éowyn) and produces a child, Elanor.

The fertility and renewed vitality of the Shire symbolize the power of restored community in its enablement of healing through love and care. Once again the king has the hands of a healer, not a destroyer. Tolkien reemphasizes his point finally by promoting Sam the Gardener to Mayor, a fertile father (Frodo envisages six children at least), and as nurturing and maternal a caretaker as any community (or master) would like.

Regal Frodo has been too wounded by his adventures to continue to participate in the vitality of the Shire, although as scholar-historian he has nearly completed the memoirs of Bilbo and himself. His point is that "it must often be so, Sam, when things are in danger: some one has to give them up, lose them, so that others may keep them" (3: 382). The sacrifice of a Frodo enables the healing of a Sam. Frodo must depart alone for the Grey Havens with the other heroes Gandalf and Bilbo, and Sam, who as Frodo admits "cannot always be torn in two" (3: 382), must return to Rose and little Elanor. This final "return"—to domesticity, simplicity, family—of the final "King" Sam reminds us that heroism is necessary to avert danger and to protect the individual, the family, and the community.

The maintenance of society, however, is best served by the caretaker and the gardener, those who keep order, nurture others, and continue the work of the family. It is their role to understand and tolerate individual difference within the community as part of that caretaking. The simple relief afforded by that lesson inheres in the final lines of *Return:*

9

Heroic Narrative and the Power of Structure

Joseph Campbell, in *The Hero with a Thousand Faces*, has designated "Departure" and "Return" the significant phases in the monomyth of the hero's quest.[48] So too do they mark the beginning and end of Tolkien's epic-romance. What the four hobbits learn on their adventures both wounds and heals them and the Shire. The three volumes, as we have demonstrated, structure those adventures in similar ways, whatever the actual focus—whether individual or community, whether politics, knowledge, or kingship. Indeed, the heroic narrative in each of the six books repeats a single structure, what might be termed the epic structure of separation from the community, descent into an underworld (read: learning), ascent into an overworld (read: grace), and the return of the individual, possibly to reintegrate within the community.

In each of the three volumes, Tolkien matches the heroic structure of the initial book to that of the second book, using the similarity to draw attention to new and different situations. Chapters 1–5 of *Fellowship*'s book 1 mirror chapters 1–3 of book 2, with book 1 suggesting a natural or literal journey through space in the present and book 2 a more figurative journey into the past. And so Tolkien stresses the natural world in book 1—that which is known and for the most part realistic (the Shire, Bree, the Old Forest, etc.)—as opposed to the supernatural, unknown, unreal landscapes of book 2 (Moria, Lothlórien, the Hill of Seeing). The hobbit world in book 1 is exchanged for the dwarf and elf world in book 2. What

Frodo especially learns in these two books differs as well. In the first, against a backdrop of natural peril (Old Man Willow, the barrow-wights), Frodo encounters the continuum of life and death. In the second book, against a historical backdrop (the history of the rise and fall of nations), he learns that moral understanding transcends merely seeing correctly and factually.

For each book Tolkien provides a similar division of chapters. To experience the separation of the individual from a community, Tolkien begins (in chapters 1-5 of book 1) with the Birthday Party during which Bilbo disappears. This is very like, in the first section of book 2 (chapters 1-3), the meeting at the Council of Elrond attended by representatives of all nations and species. In the first book hobbit "innocence" reveals the species to be childlike in its pleasures, as the second book emphasizes elven rather than hobbit wisdom. In the first book Gandalf relays to Frodo the history of the Ring (and of the hobbits); in the second book the history of the Ring is broadened to include its origin and its relationship with early peoples. The "fellowship" we see in the first book is commingled among Bagginses, Gamgees, and Brandybucks, whereas in the second it exists between all the free peoples, including elf, dwarf, hobbit, man, and wizard.

In chapters 6–8 of book 1, the natural "underworld" into which the hobbits must descend belongs to the Old Forest, or "death-in-life." In chapters 4–5 of book 2, the supernatural inferno into which the entire Fellowship must descend is the Mines of Moria, a place of past death caused by greed—spiritual death, in short. The life-in-death represented by the barrow-wights in book 1 reflects the continuing life of past civilizations, just as the spiritual monstrosity of "Durin's Bane" is epitomized by the attacking Balrog. The sleep spell of Old Man Willow (book 1) and the fog are natural narcotics akin to the darkness in the mines and at Mirrormere (book 2): one literally clouds reason and the vision; the other figuratively obviates and subverts national process, leading to greed, anger, the whole apparatus of sin.

The ascent to civilization and safety that follows this infernal experience differs as the literal differs from the figurative. The safety of the hobbits at the Inn at Bree in book 1 (chapters 9–11) corresponds to the spiritual peace and joy found with the elves in Lórien in chapters 6–8 of book 2. In contrast to the size of the Big

Folks in book 1 we are given instead the loftiness and nobility of the elves in book 2. The literal guide Strider in book 1, who will lead the hobbits safely through a threatening landscape, seems at first to be an Enemy and no friend. In book 2 the company's spiritual guide is Galadriel, who asks the right questions; she also intimidates some of the company's members by offering her mirrors as a test.

At the end of each book, Tolkien presents the dilemma of the individual Frodo, whether facing the physical danger of the Black Riders (book 1, chapter 12), or of Friend Boromir (book 2, chapters 9–10), or the psychological danger of wearing the Ring in both cases. To solve this last problem Frodo closes his eyes and rides in book 1. In book 2, in contrast, as he sits on Amon Hen (the Hill of Seeing) he opens his eyes and sees too much. Heroism is defined differently in each situation: in the first book he brandishes a sword, in the second he refuses the imprecations of Boromir and sets off, once again—alone.

What are the patterns of heroic structure in the other two volumes? In the second, *The Two Towers*, the books 3 and 4 trace the adventures of the divided company, with book 3 focusing on Merry and Pippin, Aragorn, Legolas, Gimli, and Gandalf, and book 4 focusing on Sam and Frodo. But the pattern of descent and ascent used in *Fellowship* recurs in each of these books.

At the beginning of book 3 the remaining members of the Fellowship must face the departure not of Bilbo but of Frodo and Sam, the death of Boromir in battle with the orcs, and the "departure" (actually the capture and abduction) of Merry and Pippin. Instead of hobbit history provided in a lecture by Gandalf (as in book 1), Aragorn, Legolas, and Gimli in book 3 must track those missing by means of clues and riddles. The Fellowship, though greatly reduced, uses its knowledge to succeed in locating Merry and Pippin and in summoning the key leaders of the Free Peoples to "battle" Sauron. As types of the epic hero, they do so by "descending" not into hell but into the "underworlds" of death-in-life and life-in-death.

That is, Gandalf retrieves Théoden of Rohan from his depression, his "death-in-life" caused by his twisted counselor Wormtongue, and he verbally "battles" Wormtongue into retreat. Merry and Pippin use their own hobbit cunning to escape from the "dark

Narrative Patterns in *The Fellowship of the Ring*

Book 1   *Book 2*

COMMUNITY

Chapters 1–5   *Chapters 1–3*
Birthday Party   Council of Elrond
Hobbit "innocence"   Elven wisdom
Gandalf to Frodo: history of the   Council: history of the Ring
   Ring (and hobbit history)   (and orders)
Fellowship: hobbit "orders"   Fellowship: all good orders (elf,
   Baggins, Gamgee, Brandybuck   dwarf, hobbit, man, wizard)

UNDERWORLD (NATURE)

Chapters 6–8   *Chapters 4–5*
Natural Earth   Supernatural Inferno
Old Forest: death-in-life   Mines of Moria: greed
Barrow-downs, wights (past   Balrog, orcs, etc. (spiritual
   civilizations, life-in-death)   monstrosity, Durin's Bane)
Old Man Willow's sleep spell, fog   Darkness in mines and at
                                           Mirrormere

Tom Bombadil: rescuer   Gandalf: rescuer

OVERWORLD (CIVILIZATION)

Chapters 9–11   *Chapters 6–8*
Physical safety, Inn at Bree   Spiritual peace and joy, Lorien
Big folks' size   Loftiness of elves, nobility
Strider, literal guide (landscape,   Galadriel, spiritual guide
   enemy)   (the mirror, insight)

THE INDIVIDUAL

Chapter 12   *Chapters 9–10*
Frodo: fleeing to the ford alone   Frodo: fleeing to the river alone
                                           (with Sam)

External danger: Black Riders   External danger: Boromir
Internal danger: the Ring   Internal danger: the Ring
Solution: closing eyes, riding   Solution: opening eyes on Hill
                                           of Seeing (Amon Hen)

Heroism: brandishing sword   Heroism: refusing Boromir,
                                           escaping alone

SUMMARY

Literal journey: space   Figurative journey: time
The present   The past
The natural, known, realistic   The supernatural, unknown,
                                           unreal

The cycle (four seasons)   The rise and fall of nations
The continuum of life/death   The continuum of innocence,
                                           understanding

company" of the infernal orcs led by Grishnákh. The battle at Helm's Deep takes place in a valley, an underworld vale wherein the assailing hosts of orcs and wild men attack the Deeping Wall, only to confront dwarf, man, and elf, who hew and maim the enemy. Gandalf confronts his mirror wizard self in Saruman at the prison fortress of Orthanc, where the eloquence of the latter is unmasked as seductive subterfuge, the tools of the Dark Lord, the power of the underworld.

The otherworldly help in book 3 appears in the figures of the White Rider, Gandalf, who rescues the Rohirrim from this underworld of death and devastation, and of the ents, who "rescue" and protect Merry and Pippin. Together Gandalf and the ents will meet at Isengard, the habitat of Saruman, to provide a victory for the company against the wizard imitator of Sauron, Saruman. The otherworldly help consists of wise strategy: the ents dam up Orthanc, preventing Saruman's escape, and Gandalf bandies words with Saruman to reveal his verbal perfidy. The resources at hand embody skills and wisdom that might be interpreted as supernatural. Gandalf's wizardry transcends most human (or hobbit) capabilities; the ents' mobile strength transcends arboreal abilities. These qualities, however, are characteristic not of a place like Lothlórien (as in book 1) but of individuals or species who exert leadership skills to help others. Tolkien merely hints that the ents represent some vestigial power of lost paradise in their regenerated heroism, as Gandalf, returning as the White after his deadly battle with the Balrog, appears to be a resurrected savior on loan from heaven.

In book 4 the core of the Fellowship continues on its mission while encountering adversaries and saviors equivalent to those found in book 3. To that core Gollum has been added, a dark presence like that in Book Three of the orcs to the other hobbits. This new "fellowship" will proceed through the underworld of the Dead Marshes. Here dead men and elves look outward at them to express the despair of those lost in the past, those who have failed to overcome Sauron. The "underworld" of past failure counterpoints that of present failure seen in book 3 in the debilitated king Théoden.

The overworld of the Garden of Gondor in book 4, where Faramir feeds Frodo and Sam, serves as a parallel to Lóthlorien, a true human resting place offering physical respite and psychological insight. Faramir learns that Frodo has the Ring but, unlike his brother, does not attack him; in human terms he resembles Galadriel, who also spurns the Ring.

At the end of the volume (in book 4) the miniature Fellowship is tested once again at Cirith Ungol by the attack of a dark power on the Ringbearer. Instead of the ghostly Black Riders (book 1), the human Boromir (book 2), or the cunning wizard Saruman (book 3), the chief adversary here is the giant spider Shelob, the embodiment of the primordial desire for survival. That she turns on them because of the treachery of the hungry, hobbitlike Gollum echoes the earlier treachery of Boromir in book 2, which likewise splits up the Fellowship. Here the Fellowship is so fragmented that we are left with a single hero, Sam alone.

Book 4 both mirrors and complements book 3 in that it pits hobbit against hobbit as man and wizard were pitted against man and wizard in book 3 (and as hobbit faced hobbit and man in book 1 and as Gimli and Legolas faced dwarf past and elf present in book 2). The difference between the books stems from the difference in species: both human beings and wizards desire power and knowledge, whereas hobbits desire food and comfort.

In *Return* the divided company merits divided books—all members of the Fellowship except Frodo and Sam in book 5, and Frodo, Sam, and the resolution of conflict in book 6. The two books once again reveal divided quests—one to battle (book 5) and the other to homecoming or return (book 6). But the battle is no battle and the homecoming no homecoming—that is, the Battle of the Free Peoples against Sauron (book 5) is a cover-up for the *real* "battle," of Frodo and Sam pitted against Mordor (book 6) in returning the Ring. And the homecoming of the King to Gondor and of the hobbits to the Shire unfortunately carries with it an unpleasant surprise—the revelation of Sharkey's exploitation and subterfuge in the native land, of both human beings and hobbits. This ironic reversal in each book is matched by similar kinds of inversions in the patterns of heroic structure we have observed in earlier books.

The separation from community in book 5 of *Return* involves three distinct separations—of Aragorn, Legolas, and Gimli; of Théoden, Merry, and the Riders of Rohan; and of Pippin and Gandalf. The support of a community is their natural goal, as they gather the disparate nations and peoples in preparation for the final Battle. Aragorn, Legolas, and Gimli must summon the Dead, the Oath-breakers; Théoden, Merry, and the Riders of Rohan must head for the dying city of Minas Tirith; and Pippin and Gandalf must attempt to summon back the lost mind of Denethor in Gondor.

The twin descent into the underworld in this fifth book mea-sures the darkest and most interiorized landscape—the loss of human rationality, the terrain of grief and despair, and the vortex of past failure signified by the dead Oathbreakers. Hence the "landscape" into which the members of the Fellowship descend is in actuality visualized not as a landscape but as the qualities of mind of those human beings who manifest irrationality, despair, fail-ure—Denethor and the Oathbreakers. This unusual descent is mir-rored in book 6, when the blasted landscape of Mordor serves as an objective correlative for the despair and debilitation not only of Frodo and Sam, who must fight themselves in order to continue the journey, but also of Gollum, as the non-Self who joins them, and later of the shield-maiden Éowyn, who no longer wishes to live, at least without Aragorn (and who has been touched by the Dark Pow-ers that symbolize this spiritual dis-ease).

Similarly, the entrance into an overworld here is the least obvi-ous, not associated with a place, as in other books (Tom Bombadil's house, Lórien, the Garden of the West), and most clearly internal-ized in the persons of rescuers. Indeed, that desire to serve, whether held by individual or community, marks the "paradise within" in books 5 and 6. It may be characterized as the love, loy-alty, or wisdom of a servant (Merry, Pippin, Gandalf in book 5; Sam, Gollum, and Frodo in book 6), or as the sign of natural grace (the rescue by the Eagles in book 5) that saves an entire world from disaster, or as the healing hands of a "king" (Aragorn and Sam in book 6) that restore nation or village to its past glory.

The "paradise within" does in some sense inculcate the restorative power of Lothlórien within each individual—that sense of hope, magic, goodwill, courtesy, kindness, and, most of all, spir-itual healing, which follows on all the others. Surely it is this inner strength that enables weary Frodo and Sam to battle—not only to bear, to carry, like a servant but in fact to fight—when they return to the Shire. And as heroic hobbits they represent the heart of their community: *they* are the "paradise within" that will permit a com-munity to regenerate and heal itself. And so Sam the Gardener remains as the Last Adam, intent on pruning and gardening this little pastoral paradise. If innocence has been lost, the ability to discern and shield against future threats to the Garden has been gained.

Appropriate it is, then, that Frodo departs at the end while Sam returns. The final return *is* a departure, and the final departure a return, in that Frodo himself goes "home" to familiar faces at the Grey Havens. Or, we are always departing on our heroic journeys only to discover the necessity of return—the adversary we must fight is neither necessarily external nor far away, and this adversary cannot even always be clearly recognized as such. Thus when Sam arrives home to Rosie and Elanor and acknowledges that he is home, acknowledges and accepts return, Tolkien knows the reader will understand that return merely marks a new departure and a new "journey" of the "hero," one begun again and again, endlessly and without stop. The ability to understand the cyclical nature of heroic adventure, then, is the ability to understand the necessity for locating a "paradise within." For Tolkien that ability *is* the greatest power of all.

Notes

1. Quoted in Philip Norman, "The Prevalence of Hobbits," *New York Times Magazine*, 15 January 1967, 100; hereafter cited in text.

2. For a discussion of Great Britain and World War I, see E. D. Morel, *Truth and the War* (London: National Labor Press, 1916).

3. The cold war and the public's desire for spy fiction may have helped shape Tolkien's fiction, according to Robert Giddings: see his Introduction to *J. R. R. Tolkien: This Far Land* (London: Vision Press; Totowa, N.J.: Barnes & Noble Books, 1983), which also contains Nicol Wolmsley's fine essay "Tolkien and the 'Sixties'" (73–86); hereafter cited in text.

4. Tolkien identified *Rings* as a "three-decker novel" in a letter appended to Caroline Whitman Everett's "The Imaginative Fiction of J. R. R. Tolkien" (M.A. thesis, Florida State University, 1957), 87. For the other terms, see Tolkien's "On Fairy-Stories," in *Essays Presented to Charles Williams*, ed. C. S. Lewis (London: Oxford University Press, 1947; Grand Rapids, Mich.: William B. Eerdmans, 1966), 38–89.

5. See George H. Thomson, comp., "Early Reviews of Books by J. R. R. Tolkien," *Mythlore* 41 (Winter–Spring 1985): 59–61.

6. C. S. Lewis, "The Gods Return to Earth," *Time and Tide*, 14 August 1954, 1082–83.

7. Edwin Muir, "Strange Epic," *Observer* [London], 22 August 1954, 7.

8. Orville Prescott, "Books of the Times," *New York Times*, 2 November 1954, 25.

9. Edward Wagenknecht, "Book Relates Wonderful Story," *Boston Sunday Herald*, 31 October 1954, sec. 4, p. 7; "Ring Joins Great Novels of the Year," *Chicago Sunday Tribune Magazine of Books*, 26 December 1954, sec. 4, p. 4.

10. Review of *The Two Towers*, *New Yorker*, 14 May 1955, 154, 157.

11. "The Epic of Westernesse," *Times Literary Supplement* [London], 17 December 1954, 817.

12. Charles A. Brady, "Wonderous [*sic*] Visit to Land of Dwarves and Elves," *Buffalo Evening News*, 23 April 1955, mag. sec., p. 10.

13. A[lan] N[icholls], "A Fairy Tale—but Not for Children," *The Age*

[Melbourne], 24 December 1954, 16.

14. See, for example, William Blissett, "The Despots of the Rings," *South Atlantic Quarterly* 58 (1959): 448–56; W. R. Irwin, "There and Back Again: The Romances of Williams, Lewis, and Tolkien," *Sewanee Review* 69 (1961): 566–78; and George H. Thomson, "*The Lord of the Rings*: The Novel as Traditional Romance," *Wisconsin Studies in Contemporary Literature* 8 (1967): 43–59. See also Catharine R. Stimson's brief monograph, *J. R. R. Tolkien*, published in the series of Columbia Essays on Modern Writers (no. 41, 1969).

15. See Humphrey Carpenter, *J. R. R. Tolkien: A Biography* (Boston and Sydney: Allen & Unwin, 1977, 1988), 64; hereafter cited in text. The *Crist* citation is from George Philip Krapp and Elliott Van Kirk Dobbie, eds., *The Anglo-Saxon Poetic Records* (New York: Columbia University Press; London: Routledge & Kegan Paul, 1931–53), 3: 6 (ll. 104–5).

16. For a bibliographic review on this subject, see Jane Chance and David Day, "Medievalism in Tolkien: Two Decades of Criticism in Review," in *Medievalism: Inklings and Others*, ed. Jane Chance, *Studies in Medievalism* 3, no. 3 (1991): 375–87.

17. "Guide to the Names in *Lord of the Rings*," in *A Tolkien Compass*, ed. Jared Lobdell (La Salle, Ill.: Open Court Press, 1975), 153–201.

18. See Dale W. Simpson, "Name and Moral Character in J. R. R. Tolkien's Middle-earth Books," *Publications of the Missouri Philological Association* 6 (1981): 1–5, and John Tinkler, "Old English in Rohan," in *Tolkien and the Critics*, ed. Neil D. Isaacs and Rose A. Zimbardo (Notre Dame, Ind.: Notre Dame University Press, 1968), 164–69.

19. Anthony J. Ugolnik, "*Wordhord Onleac:* The Medieval Source of J. R. R. Tolkien's Linguistic Aesthetic," *Mosaic* 10 (Winter 1977): 15–31.

20. See E. L. Epstein, "The Novels of J. R. R. Tolkien and the Ethnology of Medieval Christendom," *Philological Quarterly* 48 (1969): 517–25; William Howard Green, "*The Hobbit* and Other Fiction by J. R. R. Tolkien: Their Roots in Medieval Heroic Literature and Language," *Dissertation Abstracts International* 30 (1970): 4944A (Louisiana State University); Patrick J. Callahan, "Tolkien's Dwarfs and the Eddas," *Tolkien Journal* 15 (1972): 20; Mitzi M. Brunsdale, "Norse Mythological Elements in *The Hobbit*," *Mythlore* 9 (1983): 49–50; and Lynn Bryce, "The Influence of Scandinavian Mythology on the Works of J. R. R. Tolkien," *Edda* 7 (1983): 113–19.

21. See Mariann Russell, "'The Northern Literature' and the Ring Trilogy," *Mythlore* 5 (1978): 41–42. See also T. H. Shippey, "Creation from Philology in *The Lord of the Rings*," in *J. R. R. Tolkien, Scholar and Story-Teller: Essays in Memoriam*, ed. Mary Salu and Robert T. Farrell (Ithaca, N.Y., and London: Cornell University Press, 1979), 286–316.

22. Sandra L. Miesel, "Some Motifs and Sources for *Lord of the Rings*," *Riverside Quarterly* 3 (1968): 125–28.

23. Gloria Ann Strange Slaughter St. Clair, "Studies in the Sources of J. R. R. Tolkien's *The Lord of the Rings*," *Dissertation Abstracts International* 30 (1970): 5001A (University of Oklahoma).

24. Verlyn Flieger, "Medieval Epic and Romance Motifs in J. R. R. Tolkien's *The Lord of the Rings*," *Dissertation Abstracts International* 38 (1978): 4157A (Catholic University of America); reprinted in abbreviated form as "Frodo and Aragorn: The Concept of the Hero," in *Tolkien: New Critical Perspectives*, ed. Neil D. Isaacs and Rose A. Zimbardo (Lexington: University of Kentucky Press, 1981), 40–62. On Aragorn as healing king, see also Gisbert Krantz, "Der Heilende Aragorn," *Inklings-Jahrbuch* 2 (1984): 11–24.

25. Bonniejean Christensen, "*Beowulf* and *The Hobbit*: Elegy into Fantasy in J. R. R. Tolkien's Creative Technique," *Dissertation Abstracts International* 30 (1970): 4401A–2A (University of Southern California), epitomized in Christensen's "Tolkien's Creative Technique: *Beowulf* and *The Hobbit*," *Orcrist* 7 (1972–73): 16–20. See also Jane Chance Nitzsche, "King under the Mountain: Tolkien's *Hobbit*," *North Dakota Quarterly* 47 (Winter 1979): 5–18; revised and reprinted as chapter 2 of *Tolkien's Art: "A Mythology for England"* (London: Macmillan; New York: St. Martin's Press, 1979).

26. See Alexis Levitin, "The Hero in J. R. R. Tolkien's *Lord of the Rings*," in "The Tolkien Papers," *Mankato Studies in English*, no. 2, *Mankato State College Studies* 2 (1967): 25–37.

27. See Robert E. Morse, *Evocation of Virgil in Tolkien's Art: Geritol for the Classics* (Oak Park, Ill.: Bolchazy-Carducci Publishers, 1986).

28. Gloriana St. Clair, "*The Lord of the Rings* as Saga," *Mythlore* 6 (1979): 11–16.

29. Richard West, "The Interlace Structure of *The Lord of the Rings*," in *A Tolkien Compass*, ed. Lobdell, 77–94.

30. Derek S. Brewer, "*The Lord of the Rings* as Romance," in *J. R. R. Tolkien, Scholar and Story-Teller*, ed. Salu and Farrell, 249–64.

31. Christine Barkley and Muriel B. Ingham, "There but Not Back Again: The Road from Innocence to Maturity," *Riverside Quarterly* 7 (1982), 101–4.

32. J. S. Ryan, "Uncouth Innocence: Some Links between Chrétien de Troyes, Wolfram von Eschenbach and J. R. R. Tolkien," *Inklings-Jahrbuch* 2 (1984): 25–41, and also *Mythlore* 11 (1984): 8–13.

33. See Brewer, "*The Lord of the Rings* as Romance," 249–64.

34. Gordon E. Slethaug, "Tolkien, Tom Bombadil, and the Creative Imagination," *English Studies in Canada* 4 (1978): 341–50.

35. Ronald Christopher Sarti, "Man in a Mortal World: J. R. R. Tolkien and *The Lord of the Rings*," *Dissertation Abstracts International* 45 (1984): 1410A (Indiana University).

36. Kathleen E. Dubs, "Providence, Fate, and Chance: Boethian Philos-

ophy in *The Lord of the Rings*," *Twentieth Century Literature* 27 (1981): 34–42.

37. John Cox, "Tolkien's Platonic Fantasy," *Seven* 5 (1984): 53–69.

38. J. S. Ryan, "Death by Self-Impalement: The Prudentius Example," *Minas Tirith Evening Star* 15 (1986): 6–9.

39. Rose A. Zimbardo, "The Medieval-Renaissance Vision of *The Lord of the Rings*," in *Tolkien: New Critical Perspectives*, ed. Isaacs and Zimbardo, 63–71.

40. Verlyn Flieger, "Naming the Unnamable: The Neoplatonic 'One' in Tolkien's *Silmarillion*," in *Diakonia: Studies in Honor of Robert T. Meyer*, ed. Thomas Halton and Joseph P. Williman (Washington, D.C.: Catholic University Press of America, 1986), 127–33.

41. David Lyle Jeffrey, "Tolkien as Philologist," *Seven* 1 (1980): 47–61; revised and reprinted as "Recovery: Name in *The Lord of the Rings*," in *Tolkien: New Critical Perspectives*, ed. Isaacs and Zimbardo, 106–16.

42. Ruth S. Noel, *The Languages of Tolkien's Middle-earth* (Boston: Houghton Mifflin, 1980), and *Myths of the Ancient World* (London: Thames & Hudson; Boston: Houghton Mifflin, 1977).

43. Robert Foster, *A Complete Guide to Middle-earth from "The Hobbit" to "The Silmarillion*," rev. ed. (New York: Ballantine Books, 1978).

44. Anne C. Petty, *One Ring to Bind Them All: Tolkien's Myth* (University: University of Alabama Press, 1979).

45. Michel Foucault, *Power/Knowledge: Selected Interviews and Other Writings*, trans. Colin Wilson et al. (Brighton, Sussex: Harvester Press, 1980), 198; hereafter cited in text.

46. Cited in Norman, 100.

47. S. T. R. O. d'Ardenne, quoted in Katharyn F. Crabbe, *J. R. R. Tolkien* (New York: Frederick Ungar, 1981), 21.

48. See Joseph Campbell, *The Hero with a Thousand Faces*, 2d ed. (Princeton, N.J.: Princeton University Press, 1968).

Bibliography

PRIMARY WORKS

"Beowulf: The Monsters and the Critics." *Proceedings of the British Academy* 22 (1936): 245–95. Reprinted in *An Anthology of Beowulf Criticism*, edited by Lewis E. Nicholson. Notre Dame, Ind.: University of Notre Dame Press, 1963. Also reprinted in *The Beowulf Poet*, edited by Donald K. Fry. Englewood Cliffs, N.J.: Prentice-Hall, 1968. Contains the germs of Tolkien's ideas about good and evil, the hero and the adversary, in medieval fiction.

"On Fairy-Storie." In *Essays Presented to Charles Williams*, edited by C. S. Lewis, 38–89. London: Oxford University Press, 1947; Grand Rapids, Mich.: William B. Eerdmans, 1966. Revised and reprinted in *Tree and Leaf*. London: Allen & Unwin, 1964; Boston: Houghton Mifflin, 1965. Also reprinted in *The Tolkien Reader*. New York: Ballantine, 1966, 1975. Reveals Tolkien's ideas about fantasy and subcreation, and their relationship to recovery, in terms of Christian theology.

The Lord of the Rings. 3 vols. London: Allen & Unwin, 1954, 1955; Boston: Houghton Mifflin, 1955, 1956 (2d ed.), 1967 (4th ed.); New York: Ballantine Books, 1965 (rev. ed.), 1966.

Poems and Songs of Middle Earth. Caedmon Records TC 1231. Tolkien reads (or rather chants) some Elvish poems from *Rings*; William Elvin also sings hobbit poems set to Donald Swann's music.

The Silmarillion. Edited by Christopher Tolkien. Boston: Houghton Mifflin, 1977. As the work written before, during, and after *Rings*, it contains valuable mythological material for understanding Tolkien's masterpiece.

Pictures. Foreword and notes by Christopher Tolkien. London: Allen & Unwin; Boston: Houghton Mifflin, 1979. Selected illustrations for *The Hobbit*, *Rings*, and *The Silmarillion*, published in six calendars between 1973 and 1979 (1975 omitted).

Unfinished Tales: Of Númenor and Middle-earth. Edited by Christopher Tolkien. London: Allen & Unwin; Boston: Houghton Mifflin, 1980.

Contextual legendary history provides insights into *Rings*; an excellent index glosses names and terms.

The Letters. Selected and edited by Humphrey Carpenter, with the assistance of Christopher Tolkien. London: Allen & Unwin; Boston: Houghton Mifflin, 1981. Invaluable for tracing the relationship between Tolkien the man and Tolkien the scholar-writer.

SECONDARY WORKS

Carpenter, Humphrey. *J. R. R. Tolkien: A Biography.* London, Boston, and Sydney: Allen & Unwin, 1977, 1988. Another invaluable aid for exploring the relationship between life and letters (although it does not cite sources for its references).

Chance, Jane, ed. *Medievalism: Inklings and Others. Studies in Medievalism* 3:3 (1991): 231–392. Includes several essays (one of them bibliographic) on Tolkien's use of medieval and medievalized sources, in particular *Sir Gawain and the Green Knight.*

Cox, John. "Tolkien's Platonic Fantasy." *Seven* 5 (1984): 53–69. Reveals Tolkien's indebtedness to Platonic and Neoplatonic philosophy, especially in his definition of evil as "the privation of good, originating in individual choice."

Epstein, E. L. "The Novels of J. R. R. Tolkien and the Ethnology of Medieval Christendom." *Philological Quarterly* 48 (1969): 517–25. Shows how Tolkien's language system is based on medieval models—Rohirric on Old English, the "outer" or public names of the dwarves on Old Norse, and the Elvish languages on Welsh, Finnish, and Breton.

Flieger, Verlyn. "Naming the Unnamable: The Neoplatonic 'One' in Tolkien's *Silmarillion.*" In *Diakonia: Studies in Honor of Robert T. Meyer,* edited by Thomas Halton and Joseph P. Williman, 127–33. Washington, D.C.: Catholic University of America Press, 1986. Discusses as a starting point the influence of medieval language theory on Tolkien.

_____. *Splintered Light: Logos and Language in Tolkien's World.* Grand Rapids, Mich.: William B. Eerdmans, 1983. Studies Tolkien as a philosopher of language, especially in *The Silmarillion,* and argues for the necessity of reading *Rings* in conjunction with this early work.

Foster, Robert. *A Complete Guide to Middle-earth from "The Hobbit" to "The Silmarillion."* Rev. ed. New York: Ballantine, 1978. A helpful encyclopedia of names, places, and terms in Tolkien.

Giddings, Robert, ed. *J. R. R. Tolkien: This Far Land.* London: Vision Press; Totowa, N.J.: Barnes & Noble Books, 1983. A collection of essays approaching Tolkien's fiction from a contemporary cultural and theoretical stance.

Bibliography

Helms, Randel. *Tolkien's World*. Boston: Houghton Mifflin, 1974. Traces the development of the myth of the antiheroic hero through Tolkien's fictional works.

Hillegas, Mark R., ed. *Shadows of Imagination: The Fantasies of C. S. Lewis, J. R. R. Tolkien, and Charles Williams*. Carbondale and Edwardsville: Southern Illinois University Press, 1979. Analyzes Tolkien as an Inkling to develop his concepts of fantasy and aesthetic.

Hood, Gwyneth E. "Sauron as Gorgon and Basilisk." *Seven* 8 (1987): 59–71. Discusses the Lidless Eye of Sauron in terms of the classical myth of the Gorgon Medusa who paralyzes her victims. This myth was associated with the madness of despair in Dante's *Inferno* and also related to the Basilisk effect of the fascinator—the power of the evil ego.

Huttar, Charles A., ed. *Imagination and the Spirit: Essays on Literature and the Christian Faith Presented to Clyde S. Kilby*. Grand Rapids, Mich.: William B. Eerdmans, 1971. Examines Tolkien as a Catholic writer.

Isaacs, Neil D., and Rose A. Zimbardo, eds. *Tolkien and the Critics: Essays on J. R. R. Tolkien's "The Lord of the Rings."* Notre Dame, Ind., and London: University of Notre Dame Press, 1968. One of the first scholarly collections to examine Tolkien's artistry, specifically in relation to the quest hero, free will and fate, the Great Chain of Being and moral vision, and Tolkien's use of Old English, among other topics.

———. *Tolkien: New Critical Perspectives*. Lexington: University Press of Kentucky, 1981. Provides new critical insights into Tolkien's fiction.

Jeffrey, David Lyle. "Tolkien as Philologist." *Seven* 1 (1980): 47–61. Revised and reprinted as "Recovery: Name in *The Lord of the Rings*," in *Tolkien: New Critical Perspectives*, edited by Neil D. Isaacs and Rose A. Zimbardo, 106–16. Louisville: University Press of Kentucky, 1981. Reveals the foundation for Tolkien's ideas concerning recovery and subcreation (in "On Fairy-Stories") as the medieval concept of language, reflective of the signifying reality of the Word of God.

Lobdell, Jared, ed. *A Tolkien Compass*. La Salle, Ill.: Open Court Press, 1975. A collection of essays on such topics in *Rings* as fairy-tale morality, interlace structure, narrative pattern, and literary traditions relating to hell and paradise. Also contains Tolkien's "Guide to the Names in *The Lord of the Rings*" (153–201), which Tolkien prepared as an aid for future translators after the Swedish and Dutch translations had been published. Tolkien analyzes the etymologies and denotations of the names of persons, peoples, places, and things, derived from Latin, Old and Middle High German, Old Norse, Old English, the various Celtic languages, Dutch, and Swedish.

Mack, H. C. "A Parametric Analysis of Antithetical Conflict and Irony: Tolkien's *Lord of the Rings*." *Word* 31 (1980): 121–49. An excellent linguistic analysis of structural components, power, and language in

Rings, based on antithetical conflict and irony.

Nitzsche, Jane Chance. *Tolkien's Art: A "Mythology for England."* London: Macmillan; New York: St. Martin's Press, 1979, 1980. Identifies the interrelationship between Tolkien's scholarly essays about Old and Middle English literary works and the development of Germanic and Christian concepts of kingship and adversary in both *Rings* and *The Silmarillion* and also the minor works, including the fairy stories.

Noel, Ruth S. *The Languages of Tolkien's Middle-earth.* Boston: Houghton Mifflin, 1980. An indispensable "grammar" for Tolkien's created languages, especially Quenya.

_____. *The Mythology of Middle-earth: A Study of Tolkien's Mythology and Its Relationship to the Myths of the Ancient World.* London: Thames & Hudson; Boston: Houghton Mifflin, 1977. An encyclopedic survey of thematic antecedents (Fate and the Denial of Death), places (Middle-earth and Numenor), beings (hobbits, men, and wizards), and things (dragons and rings of power) in the Celtic, Northern, and Middle English (Arthurian), with mythological parallels in Greek, Russian, and the Teutonic.

Petty, Anne C. *One Ring to Bind Them All: Tolkien's Mythology.* University: University of Alabama Press, 1979. Analyzes *Rings* structurally in the folkloristic terms of Claude Lévi-Strauss and Joseph Campbell's monomyth from *The Hero with a Thousand Faces.*

Sale, Roger. *Modern Heroism: Essays on D. H. Lawrence, William Empson and J. R. R. Tolkien.* Berkeley, Los Angeles, and London: University of California Press, 1973. Places Tolkien in the context of modern literary heroism.

Slethaug, Gordon E. "Tolkien, Tom Bombadil, and the Creative Imagination." *English Studies in Canada* 4 (1978): 341–50. Maintains that Tom Bombadil is related to the allegorical figure Genius in John Gower's *Confessio Amantis.* The priest of Venus provides a model for Bombadil as natural conscience—plenitude, natural reason, and "ingenuity" or creativity.

Ugolnik, Anthony J. "*Wordhord Onleac*: The Medieval Source of J. R. R. Tolkien's Linguistic Aesthetic." *Mosaic* 10 (Winter 1977): 15–31. Argues that Tolkien's languages (Rohirric, Dwarvish, High-Elvish, and Common Elvish) are modeled primarily on Old English, Old Norse, and Celtic. He concludes that philology is generally the source of Tolkien's concept of fantasy: the created languages reflect the ontology and morality of Tolkien's species.

West, Richard C. *Tolkien Criticism: An Annotated Checklist.* Rev. ed. Kent, Ohio: Kent State University Press, 1981. Contains in one volume an epitome of Tolkien studies.

Index

The Author

Jane Chance is professor of English at Rice University, where she teaches Old and Middle English literature and medieval studies. She received her B.A. in English from Purdue University and her M.A. and Ph.D. in English from the University of Illinois. She is the author of *Tolkien's Art: A "Mythology for England"* (1979), *The Genius Figure in Antiquity and the Middle Ages* (1975), *Woman as Hero in Old English Literature* (1986), *Christine de Pizan's Letter of Othea to Hector, Translated, with an Introduction and Interpretative Essay* (1990), and *The Mythographic Tradition in the Middle Ages*, vol. 1 (forthcoming, 1993). She is the editor of five collections: *Medievalism in the Twentieth Century, Studies in Medievalism* 2:1 (1982); *Mapping the Cosmos*, co-edited by R. O. Wells, Jr. (1985); *Approaches to Teaching Sir Gawain and the Green Knight*, co-edited with M. Y. Miller (1986); *The Mythographic Art: Classical Fable and the Rise of the Vernacular in Early France and England* (1990); and *The Inklings and Others, Studies in Medievalism* 3:3 (1991).